MW00352087

Chief Corn Tassel

by

Mitzi Dorton

Finishing Line Press
Georgetown, Kentucky

Chief Corn Tassel

Copyright © 2022 by Mitzi Dorton
ISBN 978-1-64662-888-9 First Edition
All rights reserved under International and Pan-American Copyright Conventions.
No part of this book may be reproduced in any manner whatsoever without written permission from the publisher, except in the case of brief quotations embodied in critical articles and reviews.

ACKNOWLEDGMENTS

Thank you to my sons, Jaime and Christopher, who accompanied me on all of the little adventure trips to the historical sites of the eighteenth-century Cherokee, and to my teacher, Martha H., who always reminded me that I had this story to complete.

Publisher: Leah Huete de Maines

Editor: Christen Kincaid

Author Photo: Lana Babichenko dba Lana Ortiz Photography

Cover Design: Lynn Xue

Order online: www.finishinglinepress.com
          also available on amazon.com

Author inquiries and mail orders:
Finishing Line Press
P. O. Box 1626
Georgetown, Kentucky 40324
U. S. A.

Table of Contents

Big Rattlingourd, the nephew of Chief Corn Tassel, brother of John Watts, Jr. and first cousin of Sequoyah, possessed a great memory for the words of the elder chiefs. He approached his cousin, Sequoyah, for assistance with putting the wisdom of the old ones in writing. Although Sequoyah gave his promise, Big Rattlingourd fell sick and passed away before this was ever accomplished.

This historical narrative is dedicated to the memory of Big Rattlingourd, for this author's small contribution toward his cause. Also, to the memory of my fourth cousin once removed, H. Harold Dorton, who corresponded with me and shared ancestral stories, opening to me the world of the historic Cherokees.

INTRODUCTION

This historical narrative on the oratory of Chief Corn Tassel intends to present his life from the point of view of the person being invaded, both his and his people's effects having a cause. Like an ambassador representing the Cherokee Nation, Corn Tassel attempted at conferences and treaties to gain the sympathy and support of those attending who were capable of giving assistance. Not understanding how one could permanently own land, any more than the air they breathed, Corn Tassel and the other chiefs didn't mind sharing with the newcomers. The Chiefs had no comprehension of how the king could grant their land, when he had never owned it in the first place. The Chickamaugan Cherokee faction, not barbarian savages who enjoyed murdering for the sake of it, as white historians claimed, attempted to protect their way of life and conquer their enemy, sometimes through the law of avengement.

Corn Tassel, acting on behalf of the late eighteenth-century Cherokees, was weary with promises of restitution never carried out, yet he persevered. Presenting for him the most complex set of circumstances than for chiefs in past history, he took the office of principal chief, just as emigration brought second and third generations of the disinherited "more numerous than the stars in the skies." His office coincided with the fall of the Cherokee nation, but his methods of diplomacy are documented. Although it may emerge more than two centuries later, the story must also be viewed from the victim's perspective. Over the centuries, history, like Chief Corn Tassel and the Cherokee saga, does not stoop to deception.

Chapter I

Chief Corn Tassel was reputed to be the best statesman, as well as the greatest orator of the late eighteenth-century Cherokees. He possessed "...the inestimable character of being uniformly respected for his integrity and truth; in the last point it was said of him by all of his acquaintances, that throughout a long and useful life in his own country, he was never known to stoop to a falsehood."[1] These were the words of William Tatham, who recorded Chief Corn Tassel's speech at the Treaty of Long Island of the Holston, present day Kingsport, Tennessee, in July 1777.

In his speeches, Corn Tassel expressed his strong sentiments about the land and hunting grounds of the eastern Cherokees. However, he believed the words of his uncle, Chief Attakullakulla, that the whites were more numerous than the stars in the skies. Sir Alexander Cuming, a Scottish adventurer to America returned to Britain with a delegation of Cherokees with Attakullakulla among them, to visit King George III. Here, Attakullakulla witnessed the great numbers and shared stories of his travels with his nephew. Corn Tassel sensed with the same "appalling force the defenselessness of his own people against such an adversary."[2] It is evident that Corn Tassel retained this thought throughout his career as a friend and diplomat with the white people, this peace chief and successor of Oconistota in the principal chiefship.[3]

Corn Tassel was born somewhere in the early part of the eighteenth century, circa 1720. In reference to the infant's black downy hair, which stood straight up on his head, a family member humorously pronounced, " He is Corn Tassel." Others later teased the confident, good natured child with the round, brown face capped by a bristle of black hair, calling him "Thistle Head." Corn Tassel's grin and sprightly dark eyes manifested no objection. It was the custom of the Cherokees to give their children names, which in another society seemed to permit ridicule. However, dubbing nicknames illustrated the Cherokee's sense of humor and displayed their affection for the recipient of them. Supplementary names were bestowed throughout their lifetime as a result of an act of courage or notability. Among Corn Tassel's many names were: Thistle Head,[4] Rayetaeh,[5] Kahn-yah-tah-hee,[6] Koatohee,[7] The Tassel,[8] later Old Tassel [9](the latter two being names the white pioneers assigned to him), Onitositah,[10] and Utsidsata (Cherokee equivalent which translates Corn Tassel).[11]

Although Corn Tassel was referred to as a Cherokee, his ethnic heritage was recorded as three-fourths Cherokee and one-fourth Shawnee.[12] His mother, a fullblood member of the Paint Clan, married a half -Shawnee, who was nevertheless a chief among the Cherokees. In the matrilineal kinship system, there were seven clans, seven being a very significant and sacred number. Kinship was claimed through the mother's lineage. Corn Tassel's family distinguished themselves as members of the "An-ni-wo-di" (Red Paint) Clan by wearing feathers of a different color from those belonging to the Long Hair, Bird, Deer, Wolf, Wild Potato or Blue Clan. According to the old Cherokee law, if a person was murdered, the death would be avenged by one of the clan's members, killing not necessarily the one who committed the act, but any member of that clan. For the white pioneers, (all except those who were exceptionally revered as adopted Cherokees), they were viewed as all belonging to the same clan.

In order to strengthen him, Corn Tassel was immersed daily in water for the first two years of his life. At the age of four, under the supervision of his father, he began learning how to handle blowguns, bows and arrows. As he became older, he in turn taught his younger brothers, Doublehead and Pumpkin Boy, these same skills. When the boys matured, they went on hunting trips with the men to the Cherokee grounds in present day southwestern Virginia and into Kentucky, where they would stay for a few weeks and return with an adequate store of meat and animal skins. His two sisters, one named Wurteh, and the other whose Cherokee name translated Wind Clan, prepared meals and assisted with cultivating the fields. They performed these tasks among relatives and friends, with whom they enjoyed laughter and conversation.

The Cherokee women held prominent roles in the homes, and their opinions held strong value, both within the family and in council. Corn Tassel and his brothers and sisters revered the beloved uncles Attakullakulla, Willenewaw and Killaque, who came to visit. They enlightened the children with folklore, family history and legends. From the uncles, they possessed knowledge about the Paint and Wolf Clans to whom their family members belonged. They told of how some of their ancestors of the Paint Clan had been great medicine men or shamans. Some had practiced sorcery, masking their faces with red iron oxide paint to attract sweethearts or to protect themselves from evil persons. The Wolf Clan had been fond of wolves and raised them in captivity, training wolf pups just as dogs.[13]

Together with their cousins, Dragging Canoe and Nancy Ward, Corn Tassel and his siblings listened with intent to the remarkable stories that Attakullakulla loved to tell and retell of when, in his youth called Ookoo Naka, or the White Owl, he travelled across the great waters to meet the king of England. [Figure 1] Attakullakulla also told a story about his wife, who apparently was not as well-travelled as he, when upon hearing an organ for the first time, she insisted the lid be lifted, deeply concerned that a child might be trapped inside of it. Tame Doe, the mother of Nancy Ward (who would become the Beloved Woman and most prominent Cherokee woman of her time period), was also Corn Tassel's aunt. Standing Turkey and Old Hop were relatives as well. [See Figure 1.1]

The uncle, Attakullakulla, known as a fluent orator, was the solon of his day in the Cherokee Nation. In the Cherokee language his name translated, "Leaning Tree," probably because of his small, slender stature. William Martin, son of Joseph Martin, in the *Draper Manuscripts* described Attakullakulla as "so light habited that I scarcely believe that he would have exceeded in weight more than a pound to each year of his life." Attakullakulla was also known as the Little Carpenter because of his ability to "build bridges" in communicating and forming agreements with the whites. Samuel Williams's *Tennessee During the Revolutionary War*, refers to both Attakullakulla and his nephew, Corn Tassel, when he comments, "No other southern tribe had as able a pair of leaders, serving as contemporaries."

Corn Tassel's parents, like most Cherokee parents, were excessively fond of their children. Discipline was left to the maternal uncle, Attakullakulla. The father was not allowed to punish his children, since he belonged to a different clan. In fact, the most significant bond of the Cherokee males was not between father and son, but between the sister's sons and her brothers; while the mother had responsibility for the daughter's discipline. Therefore, the bond of Attakullakulla and Corn Tassel was that of a nature comparable to father-son, as was the bond of Corn Tassel to his nephews: Sequoyah, John Watts, Jr., Tahlonteeskee, Unakateehee and grandnephews, Robert "Bob" and Martin "The Tail" Benge.

The white pioneers criticized the Cherokee parents for "ruining" their children by being overly indulgent. However, Corn Tassel and his siblings grew up honoring their parents exceedingly and learned to respect the elders, as a part of the old Cherokee way.[14]

Corn Tassel and his siblings grew up with their parents in a longhouse, which had an opening in the roof, for the release of the smoke from a perpetual fire, kept burning throughout the winter. The pioneers referred to these as "hot houses," but the Cherokees found them comfortable. Besides his family's garden outside Corn Tassel's home, there was also a community garden that belonged to all of the inhabitants. Both the men and women worked at cultivating and harvesting. In comparison to the pioneer, the Cherokee lived comfortably, except for the fact that they had no written language to record their thoughts. One of Corn Tassel's nephews, Sequoyah, would one day change that for his people. [Figure 1.2]

As children, Corn Tassel, Doublehead and Pumpkin Boy received instruction as warriors. In addition to this training, Corn Tassel was designated a "devoted son," as he was a candidate for the chiefdom, being the oldest, the sister's son of a chief. Before presenting their child to the chiefs, his parents fasted for seven days and tasted of a certain root to bestow special powers on their "devoted son." Even though the process had initially to do with heredity, there was a selective process along the way, where Corn Tassel saw some of the candidates cast aside.[15] He seemed blessed with a gift for speaking and excelled in recalling from memory the speeches of the elder chiefs, as he listened carefully in the council meetings, and learned the ways of peace and diplomacy.

The Council House was seven sided and could seat several hundred. In the middle, at a small altar of clay, a perpetual fire burned. This was where Corn Tassel was seated on an official sopha. These sophas, or seats, were painted red in times of war, white in times of peace. People were placed on each of the seven sides according to the clan to which they belonged. Members of a clan were expected to be always both loyal and hospitable to their relatives, despite whatever differences they might have.

The Cherokee mountaineers were the largest tribe of Native Americans in the south and originally "held all the Allegheny region from Southwest Virginia to Northern Georgia, their principal towns being on the headwaters of the Savannah, Hiwassee and Tuckasegee, and upon the whole course of the Little Tennessee River, grouped in three settlements, known as the Lower, the Middle or Valley, and the Overhill towns."[16] Each section had its own dialect. The Lower towns lay in Northwestern South

Carolina, and the upper portion bordered Georgia. The Middle Settlements were located in what is today Western North Carolina. The Overhill towns were appropriately named as they were located "over the hills" from the Middle towns. [Figure 1.3] Corn Tassel and his family resided in Toqua, one of these Overhill towns, located between Chota, the Cherokee nation's capital and city of refuge, and Fort Loudon.[17]

Chota, (located in The Little Tennessee River Valley in what is now Monroe County in eastern Tennessee) was the sacred city, the most important of all the towns. Anyone could use it as a sanctuary to escape enemies. Criminals, even white pioneers, took refuge and were safe until they left its boundaries. [Figure 1.4]

Corn Tassel's "old stomping grounds" were this path of towns "along the grassy valleys and sunny slopes that skirt the southern bank of the Little Tennessee."[18] Here, he traveled south to the other Overhill towns, first to Chota, the beloved city, where he visited and ministered as leading counselor to Oconistota, the principal chief. Farther down to the Mialaquo or the Great Island and Toskegee, he conferred with his uncle, Attakullakulla, who was the Governor. Together, they parleyed over their uncertainties of having white men garrisoned at Fort Loudon among them. These chiefs, in their council meeting at Chota, anguished about the future impact of allowing a fort of this formerly unrealized magnitude, a stone's throw away from Toskegee. They wavered between arresting the establishment of it and putting their energies into a peaceful coexistence. It being so heavily garrisoned, they chose the latter.

Corn Tassel visited Fort Loudon. He knew a number of the pioneer men as political associates, and pursued friendly relations with them, inviting some to live as artisans among his people. Colonel Nathaniel Gist, also a trader among the Cherokees, and Colonel John Watts, Sr., of the garrison, took Corn Tassel's sisters as wives. Corn Tassel sincerely liked his brothers-in-law. He probably also looked upon these marriages politically, as a vehicle to maintaining peace and uniting the two races, but it went beyond that. Watts served as an interpreter for the Cherokees to the whites at the Treaty of Lochaber in 1770. Corn Tassel's attachment to Nathaniel Gist, was displayed years later at the Treaty of Long Island of Holston (in present-day Kingsport, Tennessee), where he asked that the island itself be reserved only for the use of Nathaniel Gist and the Cherokees.

Friendly relations between the Cherokees and the soldiers at Fort Loudon eventually deteriorated. According to Timberlake, Cherokee warriors aided Virginia in reducing Fort Duquense. (This was a fort established by the French at the junction of the Allegheny and Monogahela River, in present-day Pittsburgh, Pennsylvania and was then taken over by the British.) Upon their return, the warriors lost some of their horses. Accustomed to communal life, the Cherokees instead appropriated horses from some of the white frontiersmen in the same region. The Virginians resented this and killed several Cherokees.[19]

John Watts, recorded to be a man of Scots-Irish background,[20] often watched for his beautiful, dark-skinned wife, as she approached the fort with the other Cherokee wives of white soldiers, the women's laughter intertwined and similar to the sound of the bells encircling their petticoats. Their feet shuffled along in the grass, encased by their boot-like moccasins, which came halfway to their knees.

On this day, Watts watched the laughter turn to indignation and the sets of moccasins standing firm, as his wife's relative, Willenawaw, warned them that the fort was "blocked up" so that the men inside might be starved into surrendering. The women scoffed at Willenawaw, and in impudent tones, reverberated his threats with a protective furor. They told him they would continue to bring food to their husbands daily, and they made clear the intent to atone any deaths of these white "clan" members, their Fort Loudon men, for the blood of these soldiers mingled with their own half-blood offspring. Red-haired and brown eyed, dark-skinned and blue-eyed children of the Cherokee were now commonly seen running and playing along the banks of the Little Tennessee.

Willenawaw succumbed to the women's warnings, realizing it would be foolish to carry out his threats and with half closed eyes, allowed the Cherokee wives to continue bringing provisions to the fort. He was unaware that his brother, Attakullakulla, who so loved the whites, was encouraging this deliverance of provisions. Out of a certain respect for Willenawaw, and to avoid any bloodshed, the Cherokee women daily smuggled small amounts of food hidden beneath their clothing. However, the fort did eventually surrender and evacuate.

In spite of Corn Tassel's family members being quite diverse in their thinking, they respected one another in spite of it. Corn Tassel's sister, Wurteh, became the mother of the well-known Sequoyah, or George Gist, the mechanical-minded silversmith and inventor of the Cherokee syllabary. His brother, Doublehead, married Sarah Priber, the daughter of Christian Priber, a German lawyer, who wanted to establish a utopia among the Cherokees. His other sister, Wind Clan, had offspring of half Scots-Irish background, who grew up bilingual: the red-haired John Watts,

Jr. or Kunoskeeskee,[21] Big Rattlingourd, who could "rattle" off the words of the chiefs and elders,[22] and a second daughter, [23] who married John Benge, a trader of Scots-Irish background, who lived among the Cherokees all of his adult life. They became the parents of Robert "Bob" Benge (Chief Benge) and Martin Benge, who was also known as "The Tail."[24] [Figure 1.5] Bob Benge's ethnicity was as diverse as his remarkable appearance, abilities and demeanor, this tall, handsome red-haired descendant of the Cherokees, Shawnees, Scots-Irish and perhaps, the "Lost Tribes of Israel."[25]

He was known for his skill in woodcraft, speed as a runner, his dreaded name for the doom he brought for both avengement and encroachment, and yet his sometimes stunningly genteel manners with the pioneers. Bob Benge belonged to the rebel Chickamaugans, a group that broke away from the peace chief's teachings, although his personal feelings for Corn Tassel were rooted with utmost love and respect. Following broken treaties and the death of beloved Cherokee relatives, the legendary Chief Bob Benge, the Tail, and even the usually peaceful Sequoyah began to identify more with the thinking of the warrior uncles, Doublehead and Pumpkin Boy, warring members of the Chickamaugans. Described as witty and jocular in his private life, John Watts, Jr. or Young Tassel as he was called, joined his cousin, Dragging Canoe (the son of Chief Attakullakulla), took up the war hatchet and became a notable warrior and leader of this faction. The young warriors had seen the results of negotiating where the most brilliant choice of words fell upon deaf ears by those with an eye on "a big plantation way up yonder in the Cherokee nation."[26]

CHAPTER 2

In late March of 1775, a meeting was held at Sycamore Shoals, ancient treaty grounds of the Cherokee, on the Watauga River in present day Elizabethton, Tennessee. Colonel Richard Henderson, a young attorney from North Carolina, and his associates, joined by Daniel Boone were present. Boone was sought out earlier by Henderson, not only because he was familiar with most of the Cherokee headmen, but most importantly, he knew the land in Kentucky which Henderson sought to purchase. Numbering more than a thousand, various bands of Cherokees to include chiefs, dark-haired women, children and tattooed braves entered the valley, to attend the meeting.

Chieftains appeared, some dressed in matchcoats of the European style, ruffled shirts and leggings with British medals and gorgets about their chests. Oconistota, Doublehead and Dragging Canoe, whose very faces marked the white man's entry into the Cherokee world with pitted smallpox scars, were present. Attakullakulla, described by Captain Christopher French on his South Carolina expeditions, as always having a smile in his countenance, was present alongside Corn Tassel, Abram of Chilhowie, Hanging Maw, Bloody Fellow and Tennessy Warrior. Savanooka attended, his title the Raven, a tireless and successful warrior. Willenewaw, or the Great Eagle, and the Raven, were consultants upon whom Chief Oconistota depended in his decision making. Colonel Henderson, known as "Carolina Dick" to the Cherokees, announced that he would like to purchase land west of the mountains, between the Cumberland and Kentucky Rivers. Oconistota stated that their lands actually did not extend beyond the Cumberland Mountains.

Dragging Canoe was angered that the Cherokees were even participating, regardless of which tribe "owned" what part of the lands. It contained their hunting grounds. Sorely disappointed with what he heard from his elders and Colonel Henderson's proposal, Dragging Canoe jumped to his feet, the sound of his soft moccasins ornamented with porcupine quills contrasting with his deep resonate voice, as he stated with fury:

Whole nations have melted away like balls of snow before the sun. The whites have passed the mountains and settled upon Cherokee lands, and now wish to have their usurpation sanctioned by the confirmation of a treaty. New cessions will be required, and the small remnant of my people will be compelled to seek a new retreat in some far distant wilderness. There they will be permitted to stay only a short while, until they again behold the advancing banners of the same greedy host. When the whites are unable to point out any farther retreat for the miserable Cherokees, they will proclaim the extinction of the whole race. Should we not therefore run all risks, and incur all consequences, rather than submit to further laceration of our country? Such treaties may be all right for men too old to hunt or fight. As for me, I have my young warriors about me. We will have our lands.[27]

Henderson was alarmed. The chiefs themselves were so impressed with Dragging Canoe's courage, they were taken aback. Corn Tassel, wary that his people would someday be on the threshold of banishment from their own lands if they continued to yield, even wondered aloud if more consideration should be given. The cessions never seemed to satisfy, and the immediate request following was always for more land. The chiefs were then feasted again, presented with rum, spoken to individually, and shown the papers which outlined the terms of the treaty by Henderson's men. Some of the younger Cherokees, indeed, tugged on the sleeves of their elders, begging them to accept on any terms, so that they might have the wonders like scissors and mirrors that enticed them. Some of the younger men were lured too, by the guns and liquor, both unknown in the Cherokee's world, until the white man came. Although there were great divisions among the Cherokees on the issue of the transaction, the headmen began to talk as though it were in the best interest of the Cherokee to accept, for at least they would receive the goods being offered. The whites could take the land by force if they so wished. The Cherokee leaders had informed the whites that they would still have the Shawnees to struggle with as they crossed the territory. The deed was signed by Oconistota, Attakullakulla and Savanooka, acting on behalf of every one of their people. As much as Henderson was relieved to secure what signatures he could, the six-feet tall Dragging Canoe was infuriated. The land was to contain "all that tract, territory or parcel of land" lying south of the Ohio River between the Cumberland and Kentucky Rivers, an area estimated to contain twenty million acres.[28]

The Treaty of Sycamore Shoals, referred to as the biggest corporate land deal in American history, because for two thousand pounds and goods estimated to be worth the ten thousand pounds balance, the settlers had acquired almost all of the state of "Kaintuckee" and a large part of "Tanasi." Actually, Henderson was embarrassed with his six wagon loads of goods. He had not anticipated the presence of one thousand Cherokees. When the goods were distributed, one brave complained that he could kill more deer in one day on the land sold than would compare to the value of the one shirt he received as his portion.

Following the deal, Henderson announced that he had many more goods that were yet unseen with which he would like to make an additional deal. Corn Tassel looked to Dragging Canoe and noted his "I told you so" expression and folded arms. Henderson asked for a path between where they now stood and Kentucky. Daniel Boone, of the Transylvania Land Company, stood near Henderson looking pleased. Corn Tassel and Oconistota were opposed, knowing in their hearts that the Dragging Canoe's words carried truth and that the white men had taken far too much of the Cherokee hunting grounds. Oconistota displaying his agreement with Dragging Canoe at this point, stated that the whites would not be satisfied until they occupied all of the Cherokee land. The elders conferred among themselves, and it was Old Attakullakulla who persuaded Corn Tassel, Oconistota and the others to acquiesce. [Figure 1.6]. For an additional two thousand pounds, the Wataugans bought the land on which they had first illegally settled, but Attakullakulla, in sympathy, had agreed to lease to them. When the final agreement was made to do so, Dragging Canoe turned sharply to Daniel Boone and promised, "You have bought a fair land,...(but) there is a cloud hanging over it. You will find its settlement dark and bloody."

With that as his final statement at a treaty, Dragging Canoe huffed away as a Chickamaugan Cherokee and never attended another treaty. He and his Chickamaugan braves withdrew from the Overhill Towns and relocated near Lookout Mountain. In fact, he and Bob Benge, Doublehead and others would make his prediction a grim reality for the whites. It is wondered if Daniel Boone suspected it would be just as Dragging Canoe predicted. However, Boone did not seem to give it a second thought on that day. He immediately went to Long Island where he had a crew of road cutters already assembled. Each axman would get two thousand acres.[29] Faragher, author of *Daniel Boone*, remarks that in later years, the pioneer hero regretted that he had been "the instrument by which they lost their hunting grounds." Faragher paints the elderly Boone's remorse through a conversation with visitors in which Boone would question, "Through all these Trials, who do you suppose turned out to be...[my]...most constant friends? Why those very people....[I]....helped to dispossess, the Indians." [Figure 1.7]

Faragher further informs us in this biography, that Chief Oconistota took Boone aside by the hand and warned him in a friendly manner, echoing the sentiments of Dragging Canoe: "Brother, we have given you a fine land, but I believe you will have much trouble in settling it." Boone said these words indeed returned to haunt him.

CHAPTER 3

When the Virginia governor, Earl of Dunmore, heard about the huge land sale at Sycamore Shoals, he was outraged. He issued a proclamation to have Henderson leave the land, be fined or put in prison. Further, he sent word to the citizens of Watauga that they could not buy "Crown Lands" without a charter and that their purchases were illegal.[30] Corn Tassel was noted later to complain that he was "shewed" only a few pages of the proposed treaty, and that later he was told there were several, of which he was not told the contents.

Governor Patrick Henry as early as January 24, 1777, named Colonels Christian, Shelby and Preston as commissioners to negotiate with the Cherokees. Governor Caswell was tardy in choosing his representatives for North Carolina.[31] The Virginia Commissioners sent Robert Dews, a white trader, to Toqua to assess the probability of the Cherokees' willingness to come to Long Island of the Holston (present day Kingsport, Tennessee) for a conference to discuss yet another treaty. Serving as Dragging Canoe's interpreter, Dews pretended to agree with the war plans. Dragging Canoe was not only suspicious of Dews, but of the other white traders as well. Cautiously, Dews informed Dragging Canoe of the treaty meeting and tried to convince him that it would be in his best interest to attend. The son of old Attakullakulla sharply retorted, "There is no occasion for me to go; I have already heard the talks."[32]

Detrimental to Dews' purpose was a runner who appeared the following day. He informed Dragging Canoe that Colonel William Christian offered a reward for his scalp. Dragging Canoe immediately departed Toqua for Chickamauga. Dews, itching to return and warn Colonel Christian of the attitude of the war party, found that he was guarded at his every step by the watchful mistrusting eyes of the Cherokees. Frightened by a warrior who raised a gun as if to fire at him, Dews complained to Corn Tassel, who replied, "Such things cannot be prevented, the Indians regard you as a Watauga man," and Willenawaw added: "The young fellows hate you because you have come in from the woods and joined the rogues."[33]

Dews insisted upon convincing the Cherokees of his friendly intent and encouraged Corn Tassel to meet at Long Island. He offered to write and deliver two letters to Alexander Cameron, (the British agent who lived among the Cherokees), which he had been given; one from the warriors of Toqua and Tellico, and one from John Watts, Jr. to demonstrate his good will. John Watts, Jr., Hanging Maw, and a brave named Young Eagle, were later encountered by Dews at Hiwassee. There, it was discovered that Corn Tassel had already given them all of the details about the peace talks at Long Island. Dews noted that Hanging Maw referred to the white pioneers as the "Dreadful People" at Long Island. A trader among them, named Campbell quipped, "You know the King of England has many more dreadful people than the rogues," to which Hanging Maw responded laughingly, "I was only joking when I spoke of 'dreadful' people." Then he turned to Dews and said, "This man is our friend, and knows our plans, but we are not telling them to any other trader lest word get to the Virginians. They might return and destroy our towns before we can get help from the King."[34]

Colonel William Christian sent two agents, Samuel Newell and Samuel Ewing, to convince Corn Tassel to meet the colonels for a conference at Long Island.[35] Upon their arrival, Dews hurriedly rushed the men to his house, took them aside and exchanged with them the information that they had obtained on the plans of both the whites and the Cherokees. The minute Newell, described as a "pig-headed, obstinate fellow," got wind of the Cherokee plans, he angrily blurted out to the chiefs that he knew all about it. Alexander Cameron, the British agent appointed to live among the Cherokees had become influential and advised Dragging Canoe to get rid of Dews, to take his scalp and those of the other traders. The next day Dragging Canoe ordered Dews's death.[36]

Dews called upon John Benge, the white husband of Corn Tassel's niece, for information. The elder Benge was so highly revered by the Cherokees that Dragging Canoe had his own son guard him at one point. John Benge pointed to a two-gallon iron pot and informed Dews, "I believe as much Christian blood will be shed as will fill that."[37] After charging Benge with speaking "of Christian blood as though it were the blood of a bullock," Dews was told that his scalp had been demanded. Benge warned him further, "You have not a friend in the Nation, and if you can possibly escape, you had better do so quickly."[38] Dews was stricken with terror, but he had won the friendship of Chiefs Corn Tassel and Bloody Fellow, the latter named so, not because of his love for warfare, but because of a preference for rare meat. Corn Tassel sent Bloody Fellow to aide Dews in escaping. Because Dragging Canoe had demanded Dew's scalp, Bloody Fellow wrapped him in a blanket. He then led him to a thicket to hide, while he went to check the intentions of Dragging Canoe's warriors. A few hours later, he returned and accompanied his white friend to his own hot house. Corn Tassel, with the wave of the swan's wing he carried, had given the word to the warriors that Dews was to be released. Not to go against the peace headman, the warriors consented. The warriors decided to let him return to Fort Patrick Henry with the Raven. Dews became aware of "the staunchness of Indian friendship."[39]

The two Samuels, Newell and Ewing, were not successful in inducing Corn Tassel to meet at Long Island of the Holston for a conference. In January of 1777, Newell returned again to convince Corn Tassel and lost his life at the hands of the original people on his way home.[40]

CHAPTER 4

General George Washington recommended Nathaniel Gist be commissioned as colonel in the continental army. He was chosen because of his known friendship and influence with the Cherokees to bring them to the promised treaty at Long Island. Gist sent a letter to Oconistota, the Raven, Dragging Canoe and Corn Tassel and informed them that it was "the last offer of peace" they "would get from Virginia." This letter, dated March 28, 1777, thought to be Dragging Canoe's copy, ended up in the British Archives in London, and was published in Appendix A of Samuel Williams' *Tennessee During the Revolutionary War*. [Figure 1.9] Because of their utmost regard for and trust in Nathaniel Gist, and their fear of being outnumbered in a war, a number of chiefs did relent and travel to Long Island to treat. Corn Tassel, Oconistota and Attakullakulla were among them. Such was Colonel Gist's influence that he convinced Oconistota and some other chiefs also to meet with Governor Patrick Henry at Williamsburg.

The Long Island Treaty Conference (present day Kingsport, Tennessee) was held March 20, 1777 with the three Virginia commissioners in attendance. There were still no North Carolina commissioners present. Although Gist's influence was great with the Overhill chiefs, his letter was ignored by Dragging Canoe. Without Dragging Canoe's presence, they decided to reschedule the negotiations until June of 1777.[41]

The purpose of the Treaty of Long Island, from the white settlers' point of view, was to extend the western boundary of Virginia and provide a legal pathway for the settlers to emigrate to Kentucky. John Donelson, in 1772, had run what was known as "Donelson's Line," and there was much controversy about its borders between the white settlers and the Cherokees.[42]

It would be ten days before Corn Tassel would set foot upon the familiar beloved Long Island, (present day Kingsport, Tennessee), where his forefathers met and smoked their pipes of peace. On June 30, 1777, Oconistota, the "ancient chieftain" referred to as the "chief king or emperor" of the Cherokees[43] by the white men, entered the old and sacred treaty ground. Colonel Christian, a Virginia commissioner, had escorted him to Williamsburg with an accompaniment of Native Americans, many of them warriors who had followed their old chief or "uku."[44] Within minutes, the commissioners from North Carolina were in attendance. Waightstill Avery and William Sharpe, who both studied law, arrived, plus two militiamen, Robert Lanier, who had been a colonel in the Revolutionary army and Joseph Winston, a major in the North Carolina militia.[45]

On July 2, one of these warriors, Big Bullet, (a mixed blood son of John McCormick, one of the interpreters, and a Cherokee woman), waded out to a small island and sat there, mending his moccasins, never aware that a white man crept stealthily within rifle range. Seconds later, Big Bullet fell dead, and the camps were upset. The peaceful camp suddenly became armed on both sides. The Cherokees were not the only fearful ones, for the white men were also uneasy, afraid that their chances of negotiating a treaty that would open up new lands would now be jeopardized. Both sides were angry, and violence was about to break out.

Chief Oconistota had "a powerful frame and in his prime must have weighed over two hundred pounds, having a head of enormous size."[46] Oconistota, or Groundhog Sausage, as his name translated in English, was noted to avoid speaking in public when he could do so as he claimed his powers of oratory were weak.[47] However, since Corn Tassel and the Raven had not yet arrived, he spoke to the commissioners. Oconistota related that the governor had told him "that no man should break the Belt given me by him….but the white people….have struck me and spilt Blood about the chain unknown to my father." After expressing his dismay that the recent talk had already been broken, he expressed the desire that peace continue and "not spoil the goods Talks." He credited this mishap to a "verry (sic) bad man" and said he should "look upon it as an accident."[48] It was his opinion that the British agents, Alexander Cameron and John Stuart," would laugh and be pleased at it," but he did "not care for what they can say." He would tell his "own people not to mind Cameron's & Stuart's Talks" as he had told them he was "done with them and all the talks they give…."[49]

Oconistota feared that the young warriors, alarmed by the news of Big Bullet's death, would bring about bloodshed, but stated, "I shall say the same to the warriors who I expect every day; and desire them not to mind it was done by a verry (sic) bad man." As a helpless admonishment he added,

"This is the second time such an accident has happened, but it shall not make us think the least hard of it." The Commissioners assured Oconistota that they were "all heartily grieved." They added that they hoped it would not spoil the good talks, and offered a string of wampum. Subsequently, a six-hundred-dollar reward was posted on the front gate of the fort to any person discovering the murderer of Big Bullet. The murderer was not actively sought however, and even though it came to light that Robert Young was the culprit, the Virginia soldier was never held accountable.[50]

On July 4, 1777, the fort atmosphere became quite festive in celebrating the anniversary of the Declaration of Independence. The white soldiers paraded about and fired their guns. The Cherokees were presented gifts of whiskey, and the young warriors closed the entertainment with a dance. From this time until July tenth, numerous chiefs with small parties arrived. Chief Corn Tassel referred to as the "Old Tassel" or simply "The Tassel" by the white men, came in on this day.[51] On the same day, Savanooka, or the Raven of Chota (Oconistota's nephew) arrived, followed by Willenawaw. Both were not only political associates, but relatives of Corn Tassel. Chief Oconistota "made it his business to attend and listen to what passed in all treaties; and he took care to preface them with a candid acknowledgement that he was no speaker and not much of a statesman."[52] Because of his age, Oconistota resigned his power to Corn Tassel and the Raven, but always added that if they should speak contrary to his own sentiment, he would "put them right."[53]

Several speeches were given by various chiefs that dwelt on the death of "The Big Bullet," saying however that they imputed no blame to any but the individual offender who committed the act.[54] Corn Tassel sat with his head stationed in a lofty manner with a whitened deerskin wrapped about his shoulders awaiting his turn to address his white "elder brother." He hoped they could come together with an agreement to unite both the original and white people in peace and friendship. A silver engraved medal hanging around his neck signified this was not the first time he had negotiated in some manner with the pioneers. His otter skin cap, covered with the snowy down of a swan and wreathed with upright swan feathers, gave him a majestic appearance. To complement his regal Native American aura, he carried a wand of swan wings.[55] Corn Tassel was a "stout man, mild and decided." He was "rather comely than otherwise,"[56] suggesting that in his youth he was a handsome fellow, but now his face was "somewhat fat and inflated,"[57] a condition perhaps accompanying his longevity.

All of the speeches of Corn Tassel and other chiefs will be recorded with the spelling, capitalization, punctuation (or lack thereof), as the pioneer originally transcribed them.

CHAPTER 5

Corn Tassel's first recorded speech at the Treaty of Long Island involved the experiences of which he was told by the "Norward Indians." The Americans had asked him to tell all that he knew concerning the state of mind, deeds and travels of the northern tribes. Corn Tassel was anxious to share this information, because he felt that the actions of these other tribes had been blamed on the Cherokees.

In his diplomatic manner, he expressed to the white people his own feelings, using to avoid conflict, what these Indians related to him. Captain White Eyes, to whom he refers, was head of the Delaware Nation and a friend to the Americans, maintaining a neutral position between the Americans and the British. Chief Cornstalk, of the Shawnees, also held a neutral position at this time and sought to maintain peace with the Americans. Like the pacifist Corn Tassel and the Chickamaugans, some of Cornstalk's people fell in with a remnant faction, a militant band that had its own agenda.

The Notawagoes, or Nottaway were originally found by the Virginia colonists on the Nottaway River. They were a mixed band of Iriquois, Savannah, and Conestoga, their closest connections being Meherrin, Tuscarora, Nanticokes and Susquehanna. During the Revolutionary War, the Nanticokes joined the Cherokee Chickamaugan forces and fought on the side of the British. The Twightees were a part of the Iriquois and Ohio Indians. The Twightes, Delawares, Shawnees and Wyandots had attended a treaty together with Ben Franklin in 1753. The Mingoes of whom Corn Tassel speaks allied themselves with the British, Shawnee and Wyandots. It was complex, not only which faction represented the tribe, but the identity of the remnants who joined together as one. These were some of the "Norward Indians."

Chief Corn Tassel:

My Brothers may be certain I will tell them the truth. It was but the other day we were talking together when we promised we would tell all we knew to each other. I will now tell all I now (sic) about the Norward Indians that lately came to Chote, as their talk was to me. These mingoes came in after Vanns express arrived. They had met with the second man of Chilhowey (sic) on his way here, and he turned back to them as follows.

Brothers, I am Glad to see you once more; we have been at war and making Peace several years. Last year you came here and told me lies from your council, which did me and my people great hurt. But now I make you welcome; but your stay must be short. (I gave them a small string and told them this was the beloved Town where the Warriors speak together.) I see by your looks that your hearts are bad, and that you have been doing mischief as you came here. I gave you this string that you may tell the truth. I am now going to the beloved men at the Island where our talks with the white people are good, and not as they used to be. You are come now contrary to my expectation. Some of your people came here last year and told lies, and set me and my people at war with a people that I never intended to be at War with; and it looked as if my Nation were but like one House against them. It was but the other day I was at the Island making Peace with my elder Brothers and all your bad Talks shall not again spoil it. I am now talking with you who I have called my elder Brothers. I find the days dark between you and the white People; but that shall not spoil my good Talks. You may kill a great many of them, even four, five, or six thousand and as many more will come in their place. But the red men cannot destroy them. Your lies made me have the short trouble I had, but I am now carrying on good Talks and all you can say shall not prevent them. And I hope you will soon be doing the same, as our elder Brothers are verry (sic) merciful to our women and children. They then answered

Brothers we are only come to see you and not to hold talks. When we left our Towns all the Northern Tribes were ready to strike the white People. Only one man desired them to wait untill (sic) he would go to the Lakes and see the white people there. We have been forty days on our Journey (sic). Sixty of us set out together from our Towns and on our way attacted (sic) a Fort on Kentuckie (sic) where we lost one man and got two scalps. We left that Fort and attacted (sic) another small one, but no damage was done on either side that we know of. We (sic) then parted and forty-nine went home; and we came to see if the Cherokees were cut off as had been reported. But we are now in haste to return to meet the

Indians who are to invade the frontiers from this River to the Forks of Ohio. The Western Tribes have all been spoken too (sic); and that Northern Tribes are all ready for War. The Nottawagoes had been spoken to by a great Town of white people far off, perhaps Queebeck (sic), who said "will you be always fools? will you never learn sense? "don't you know there is a line fixed between you and the white people, "that if they set their foot over it you might cut it off; and if they turn and set their heels over, you might cut them off also? Now they have come over the line and encroached on your lands and why will you suffer it? Don't you understand this?" These Indians then agreed this was truth, and immediately sent runners through all their land amongst all their Tribes, who agreed to send a few of their Warriors to strike the Blow, and then the white people might follow if they please, and go amongst them, and try to cut them off as they have done the Cherokees. These Nottawagoes instantly sent out some warriors who killed two white men and then returned, and a large Body of them were about to set out a second time; but the white people might follow if they please, and go amongst them, and try to cut them off as they have done the Cherokees. These Nottawagoes instantly sent out some warriors who killed two white men and then returned, and a large Body of them about to set out a second time; but the white people at the great falls (perhaps Niagara) said they should not go out untill (sic) they would give them a writing on paper to lay on every mans (sic) Breast they should kill, that the white people might know the reason of it. We were told by some Twightwes that a large Body of their people had set out to kill white people, and on our way here above the Falls of Ohio we saw signs of them returning with a vast number of Horses they had taken from the white people, and we dont doubt but they have done great Damages (sic). The Nottawagoes said if the white people comes (sic) out against you they will be discovered as your men are always in the woods, then you must give us notice and we will come and fight them. There are three towns of the Shawnese & Delawares where the Cornstalk and Captain White eyes lives (sic), whom we have spoken to and told them it was verry (sic) well for them to carry on their good Talks with the white people, for that these Towns & us had no connections. The Nottawagoe Warriors came to two Delaware Towns with Belts, and told them "they had agreed to go" to war with the white people and desired that they might move off, "least in the war they might be trod down by them, or the white people. "That they did not want them to join; but they must remove beyond "the mingoes, to be out of their way. And they might still carry on "their good Talks with the white people." They also spoke to Capt.

"White Eyes and told him he was a great [chief?] and a warrior. "That they had given him the beloved Fire, and it gave them great "trouble to ask him to remove, as he was dreadful amongst the red men; "for fear something might come out of the ground which would put "out that fire." This is all we can tell you which we can assure you is the truth. In the last part of the Talk they said "You are now making "peace for the security and safety of your Nation." We do not want "your assistance. If we suffer, we will bear the loss ourselves, for we "are looking for it, and deserve it; as our young men are determined to "go to war and try the white men. It may be that we and our elder "Brothers may yet talk together of Peace, and we will keep hold of the "friendship we have with the Cherokees, but we desire no assistance "from them, as we did not give them any when they were in trouble."

I told the road they must take which was down the Little River and through Cumberland gap; and that they must not hurt any white man on this side of that mountain, least it would destroy the good talks that were going on. But now I am convinced that it was them that did the mischief the other day (meaning the captivating Cash Brooks about thirty miles from this place.) and not my people, for as I came up, I looked where they should have crossed the river as I directed them, but could not discover sign of them."[58]

In an attempt to prevail upon the Cherokees a state of contentment, the Virginia Commissioners mentioned the presence of the well-loved white man, Nathaniel Gist, who was the father of Corn Tassel's nephew, Sequoyah. The commissioners addressed the Cherokees saying, "We…are rejoiced to see you once more sitting around the council fire…We on our part are pleased to see that our common friend Colo. Gist….who went into your country….returned safe" and was "well treated…." Referring to the Chickamaugans, they stated, "We hope your young men have seen their error and that for the future will listen to the advice of their fathers and the old wise men and pay no regard to any bad men….who will….engage your Nation anymore in a war with your elder Brother the white people…."[59]

Corn Tassel's sensation of pride in his association with Colonel Gist shifted to anxiety when the commissioners expressed their regret at the absence of his nephew and namesake, John Watts, Jr. or Young Tassel. He also was displeased with the actions of the young men and wished they would heed the advice of the older ones. He recalled his conversations with the warriors, where he admonished them to cooperate with the white people. While he grasped their anger at empty promises and broken treaties, he could not understand why these young men, who had been told and retold since very young, the stories about the travels of Attakullakulla, then called "Leaning Tree," when he sailed across the great waters to England. Attakullakulla was always quick to emphasize the numbers of white people he witnessed in England. Yet, the young men persisted in their thinking that negotiating was foolish and fighting was the only answer. Corn Tassel was highly loved and regarded by these young men, but they did not accept his way of peace and what he deemed compromise.

The commissioners continued to assert the purpose of this meeting was for "peace...so strong... and so lasting that our children yet unborn may enjoy the blessings and benefits of it...." They expressed their sorrow for the absence of "Judge" Friend, The Dragging Canoe, the Lying Fish and Young Tassel. "Judge" Friend actually meant Judd's Friend or Ostenaco. He was known to the colonials as "Judd's friend" as early in his career he had saved a trader named Judd from being harmed from Cherokee anger. The Lying Fish, or Utsutiganagohi, was a seceding headman from Toqua, and Young Tassel was Corn Tassel's nephew, John Watts, Jr., and along with Dragging Canoe, part of the Chickamaugan faction.

The commissioners said, "We are fully authorized by the Governor of Virginia to fix a Boundary between your country and the white people, and to settle a firm peace with your Nation for the benefit of your people... In the meantime, we have had the pleasure of talking with your beloved men... and seeing your young men eating, drinking and dancing with our young men like friends and Brothers. We are verry (sic) sorry that Judge friend, the Dragging Canoe, the lying Fish and young Tassel (John Watts, Jr.) are not come to the Treaty as we expected they might have been of use in your Country...."[60]

Chief Corn Tassel hoped that the meeting was being held for the sole purpose of bringing peaceful relations and good will to the two races, by removing the encroachers, but he strongly suspected from past experience there would be some requests made by the commissioners. Corn Tassel began,

> Now you shall hear what I have to say to my elder
> Brothers. It seems as fresh in my mind as if it was only two nights
> ago since we had our last Talk. Our beloved man has been to
> see your beloved man of Virginia. Now I have seen you my elder
> Brothers which makes me glad and its (sic) augmented by our
> beloved mans (sic) return to us. I have now fast hold of you by
> the hand and will not let loose my hold. I am now verry (sic)

thankful to the powers above that the people of my Elder
Brother and my own people are now got here to this place;
a place which I have come to with all my people to make all
things straight. My heart is good to all my Brothers, but I am
sorry I have been a little short in coming here. There was (sic)
so many days appointed for my beloved man to go and see our
beloved elder Brother and likewise to return in, which they
did not according to the appointed time, but now we are here
together in order to make all things straight. Yesterday you and
I had Talks together, you said it was what I would to bring on
the business, which I do not desire because you are the elder
Brothers. All our principal men are now here and tomorrow
morning if you please you may bring on the principal Talks.
There are many people desirous to return home again, and I
would be glad how soon the business might come on that they
may go to work in their fields which are now suffering for want of
Labour (sic).

A string of Beads[61]

(The person who presented a string of white beads expressed a wish for
peace, truthfulness and mutual happiness.)

The Raven, Corn Tassel's co-speaker, "was by birth a Shawanee; (sic)
but by marriage, he belonged to the Cherokees with whom he resided; and
he was the hereditary representative of the Cherokee empire."[62] He spoke
after Corn Tassel expressing his hope for future generations:

This is the bright chain of friendship which we have
hold of, not only us but the young ones on both sides, even the
children yet unborn have hold of it through us, and shall be fast
linked together by it….it is a light for those yet unborn to walk
by, that they might see the path of peace and know what is done
at this place….Three beloved men are talking together Virginia,
Carolina and Chote all talking the peace talks together….I believe
that long before my remembrance this land was first found
out, the time you know as you have writings….before my
remembrance, by the time these meddles (sic) were given to us
(shewing a meddle) (sic) ever since these have been among us we
have been more and more distressed….[63]

Perhaps at this moment, the other chiefs glanced down at their own silver engraved medals with which all their chests were similarly adorned, and wondered how many times "peace" would be offered. The Raven continued,

> The beloved man which I had in my land some time
> ago used to give us talks which I thought were verry (sic)
> good, but I believe now they were bad and never went to you....
> He told us that when we found any of your people on our land
> to take their guns, Horses and everything they had and if we
> killed them no harm would come of it, which advice I followed
> and it had liked to have been my ruin....[64]

Following the Raven's oratory, Corn Tassel rose, shook hands with the commissioners, then spoke complaining that they need to be given "a little room, because your people have encroached upon us verry (sic) close and scarcely given us room to turn around."[65] Corn Tassel stated:

> It is the third moon since we first took hold of each
> other's hand, which was ordered by the Great man above, and
> you remember what talks we had together; I spoke freely from
> my heart that it might sink deeper into yours; as we were making
> the peace when I was here before, my friends you said this was
> the bloody path, I have swept it clean, and it shall no more be
> thought of. You likewise said that all the flesh wasted on both
> sides should be thought of no more, but as if they had been
> burried (sic) so long ago that a large tree had grown upon the
> grave. Twas you and me had this talk when we were counseling
> in peace. It shall be an everlasting peace. It was so ordered by
> the great man above and for that reason we will be the last to
> break it, altho (sic) a wicked white man did spill a little blood (a
> reference to Big Bullet) which shall no more be thought of. Now
> all my elder Brothers have heard both beginning and end of our
> Talks. I expect there will be interruption (sic) for any of either
> people to go where they please. These beads are for Colo. Gist to
> take to the Norward
>
> A string to Colo. Gist[66]

(Andrew Williamson, to whom Chief Corn Tassel refers in the following speech, led numerous campaigns against the Cherokee. The

"Unacay" Mountain, as the interpreter transcribed was intended to be the Unaka Mountains on the border of Tennessee and North Carolina.)

> I remember what you said concerning the letters from Colo. Williamson who I know verry (sic) well, I heard all you said on this matter before, and also that Colo. Williamson had been through all our Country and that he wanted the land as far as the Seneca. I remember all the talks which my people said they had with Colo Williamson. When he said he wanted the land as far as the Unacay Mountain, our people said they would consider of it. I live in Toquoe and my beloved people in Chote, we did not go far away and came back again these middle settlement people did so too, and I dont see how they can claim the land by that, for we drove the white people from their houses too. Many of their people have been to that treaty but chiefly women and children they returned from there naked as my hand and crying with hunger by which it appeared that they only wanted our land and not to make peace. The beloved men of Virginia now here I suppose are good men sent by their Great beloved man. I think the same of my Brothers of North Carolina. Now I hope your Great beloved men will take pity on us and do us justice, as our provisions is (sic) chiefly destroyed, and give us a little room, because your people have encroached upon us verry (sic) close and scarcely given us room to turn round (sic). I've been talking with the beloved men of Virginia, and I hope nothing will break the good talks we have had together. My Brothers of North Carolina were not here before to hear the good talks, but these they hear and I hope all three of us will observe them.[67]

Williams recorded Tatham's pen sketch of the Raven of Chota or Savanooka: This chief "was a stout, manly, firm and dignified person; of an open, yet serious deportment, dark complexion, steadfast and comely countenance; and was reputed to be the most powerful man in the Cherokee nation at athletic exercises. He bore the reputation of a good warrior, and certainly was not inferior in council or oratorical abilities to any one of his tribe."[68] He wore a raven skin around his neck.[69] While Corn Tassel was speaking, the whiskey the Cherokees had received as a gift, left about four hundred of them encamped on the opposite island severely

inebriated. Such was the outrageous behavior in camp, that the Cherokee women began to busily employ themselves in hiding guns, tomahawks and other weapons. Tatham informs us that "the whole
encampment had become a scene of riot and confusion which disturbed the spectators of the treaty."

Corn Tassel ceased speaking for a moment, cuing the Raven, who in turn arose from his seat. He directed two young warriors from the audience to the rioters. In seconds, they were in a canoe, crossed the river, quieted the camp, as though its occurrence were a figment of the imagination, and rejoined the audience with no further interruptions."[70]

Williams remarked in his biography of Tatham "that such an affray would have been harder to quell under the boasted regulations of a civilized system, yet these were savages![71] (Perhaps he should have ended his sentence with a question mark.)

CHAPTER 6

The Raven of Chota or Savanooka spoke to the Commissioners:

I understand from my friend it was by the old Great Man over the water that my land was settled; but I know nothing of it. The time is fresh in both our memories when he was sitting on the Throne and if the land ever belonged to him its more than I know of. You and I were talking last night on the subject of the Boundary line and I told you what I thought was a proper place. You propose a line that goes beyond what I mentioned and binds verry (sic) close upon me.

Mr. Avery responded:

"…Many years ago the Governor of North Carolina, who you called the Big Wolf, Governor Tyron, agreed with your Nation, and fixed a line between your and our people…our Governor and Council did order any settlement, to be made over that line. If any such had been made without your consent, you ought to have complained to our Governor and Council…."We desire in behalf of the State of North Carolina, that a line should now be agreed upon, between your Country & our Country that you for the future shall not consent….We are about to fix a line that shall remain through all generations…. *We shall recommend it to our Governor… to make laws to punish any white man, who shall settle or encroach on your lands or in any manner injure or disturb you.* By fixing a line and abiding by the same, we may be lasting…."

Mr. Avery continued,

We desire to know your opinion whether you think it would be just to remove the inhabitants of Watauga and Nolachuckey (sic); or whether you do not think it would be better…to fix a boundary, below our inhabitants, beginning at the ford on holston (sic), where the path crosses at the lower end of the valley, running thence a straight course towards a point about three miles below Cumberland Gap, until it intersects the line hereafter to be extended between the States of Virginia and North

Carolina; and from the said ford, a straight line towards Nolachuckey River five miles West of the mouth of McNamies Creek thence South, crossing Nolachuckey to the Southern bank thereof & from thence South East into the mountains, which divide the Hunting grounds of the Overhill Towns from those of middle settlements.

A String[72]

Corn Tassel's ears were cut and beaded in the Cherokee fashion with silver hanging nearly down to each shoulder, bobbing as he shook his head "nay" in response to the North Carolina Commissioner:

July 15, 1777

I look upon it the line you ask is much too nigh to my Nation it takes in all your settlers on Nolachuckey River, which are themselves too nigh; but this shall not spoil our good talks.... I want liberty to raise my children and have an open Country. I speak freely because I have a right to speak in my own behalf. This line I cannot agree to, as it is too near my Nation; nearer I believe than you think for. For I look upon it you would not make an unreasonable demand. I am verry (sic) thankful for the many good talks between us for the safety and security of my people; but did not expect you would talk of boundaries so near my Towns. It seems as if my elder Brothers speak with a stranger mouth than I can, but this argument seems weak when set against what I say, for that line is too near me. I believe my elder Brothers want to know my principles. I thought they had known them before. I was never guilty of telling lies, all my people depend upon my word; and I tell you none of them have a bad heart against my Elder Brothers at this time. This is all I have to say this evening upon the subject, tomorrow I will speak again.[73]

Chief Corn Tassel had labored for two moons over a response that would make the commissioners take notice and realize that his people were human and greatly affected by the results of these requests. He was dressed in a white shirt of the English make.[74] His breeches, extending halfway to the knees, were fastened with a leather belt, that reached twice around his waist, and from which hung long tassels, swaying at his thighs when he arose to speak. The matching tassels hanging from the garters under his knees, danced back and forth as he stepped forward to address the "elder brothers," and his white moccasins, with small bells attached and jingling, announced his presence.

July 17, 1777

Now the beloved men of North Carolina shall hear my reply to what they said to me last night. The talks you gave me came from the Governor to make a path from your Country to mine and was verry (sic) good till (sic) you came to talk of the boundary line. My beloved man and the beloved man of Virginia have taken hold of each other fast high up the arm.

It may be the same by my brothers of North Carolina. But by their asking so much land it seems as if they want to see what we would say, that we might refuse something, and they might catch us in a trap for an excuse. I left people both at home and in the woods far beyond there, who are waiting and listening to hear what I do. As you are talking of much land I don't know how they would like that part of your proposal. As I said beloved men are here together. My beloved Man (sic) has been to see the Great beloved man of Virginia who I suppose wrote to your Great beloved man to send you here, and talk about making Peace. I want to know whether he wrote anything to him to require so much land as you seem to do. I am talking to my Brothers so I call you all. as to land I did not expect anything on that subject; but only concerning peace. The man above hath ordered it so that the white benches shall be set down for us, and I hope nothing will enter either of our hearts but good thoughts. I would leave it to the beloved man of Virginia to settle all things (about Lands) between us. I am talking with my elder Brothers on a subject I cannot clearly comprehend. I did not expect it would have been put to me at this time; for my elder Brothers have imposed much on me in the land way.

If this and another house was packed full of goods they would not make satisfaction. But I will leave the difference between us to the great Warrior of all America. It seems misterious (sic) to me why you should ask so much land so near me. I am sensible that if we give up these lands they will bring you more a great deal than hundreds of pounds. It spoils our hunting ground; but always remains good to you to raise families and stocks on, when the goods we receive of you are rotten and gone to nothing.

Your stocks are tame and marked; but we dont know ours they are wild. Hunting is our principle (sic) way of living. I hope you will consider this and pity me. Here is my old friend the Elk (meaning Colo. Preston) and two particular from Virginia hearing the answer I make to my brothers of North Carolina.

you require a thing I cannot do, for which reason I return you the string of Beads to consider upon again. In my talks at Chote Town house there shall be nothing bad towards my elder Brothers. I will hold them fast and strong. I have often been told that my elder Brothers were naked and had nothing. I said if so I will be naked also. I looked for nothing but to raise my children in peace and safety. My former friend who is now my Brothers enemy told me if I listened to you I would wear hickory bark shirts; but that Talk I do not mind.

returned the String

Then the old Tassel spoke to the Virginia Commissioners as follows.

I am going to speak to my friends and elder Brothers who I hope will remember what I am going to say. Ever since winter the good talks have been going on between us. Here is the Raven who first came to us with the good talks. Your second messenger happened to be killed by some of our bad people, who were not at that time well to my elder Brothers, and it was a great grievance to me. When the Raven came here last winter it was proposed to him by my elder Brothers, that a great and good warrior would go with him into the Nation; but this he objected to for fear some bad people would accidently (sic) meet with him, and kill him. In that case the Raven said "he must die also." Then another man was sent with him, for which I am verry (sic) thankful to my elder Brothers, in that they left the good Warrior with his own people. Now I have got this good Warrior fast by the hand, and will lead him to the beloved seats in Chote, where he shall sit down and keep the beloved talks, between me and my Elder Brothers. I'll take him and lead him through all the Towns in safety. He shall sit down and smoke with my beloved man, and hold the chain of friendship hard and fast, that nobody shall pluck it from him, as I have him by the hand and determine never to let him go. I hope my elder Brother will never be sorry that he is gone with me. As he is a good man to you he will be the same to us. Any News that comes to us there of any kind, and from any place he shall send it here to this seat of Justice, that my elder Brothers may know it.[75]

Colonel Christian then referred to their earlier meeting on the island when the "Great Warrior's" (General George Washington) letter came to "Brother Oconistota" reminding the Cherokees that they were treated well and clothed during their stay. He stressed the increased size of General Washington's army and the success of his battles. Col. Christian commented on the benefit of Colonel Gist's friendship to the Cherokees in bringing peace between the two races. He subsequently requested that Colonel Gist, as "he has long been a friend to your Nation....to let some of your Warriors and young men accompany him to the Northward, as they can safely trust themselves with him." Then Colonel Christian mentioned the Cherokees could have "the opportunity of traveling through an extensive, rich and populous Country...."viewing "the Grand of thirteen United Countries, in the Great City of Philadelphia, and at the General's camp, "seeing "the finest and largest Army that ever was in America...."[76]

To which Corn Tassel replied:

> Here is my friend and Brother (pointing to Col Gist) whom I look upon as one of my own people. He is going to leave me and travel into a far Country, but I hope he'll return. Here is one of my people the Pidgeon (sic) that will accompany him but I do not know of many more that will. He will think no trouble of the journey it is all by land and will seem light to him. He once went over the Great Water where he could not see which way he was going; but this journey will be all by land and he will think nothing of the fatague (sic). I am verry (sic) thankful that such a man as the Pidgeon (sic) has undertaken this journey; because we think much of him, and I rely that my friend will take care of him. I cannot be accountable how many men will go with the pidgeon (sic) and my friend; I (k)now (sic) of only three or four there may be more but will see at night. Now this is the last talk I have to give. We have been long here and some of my people are desirous to go to the cornfields which may be on sufferance for want of labour.
>
> Tomorrow I am very sensible some of them will set out. I want the talks over myself as soon as possible; but I know matters of great consequence cannot be hurried on. I hope the business

will get so far done that I may go in three days. But we will see one another often times at this place where the beloved fire is left.

A string to Colo. Gist

Corn Tassel continued his speech, mentioning traders, Ellis Harlan, Sr., Joseph Vann and George Lowrey. Ellis Harland, Sr. was a white trader, who married, Ka-ti, and Captain Joseph Martin, who married Betsy, was the "beloved man holding the good talks," to whom Corn Tassel initially refers. Both Ka-ti and Betsy were daughters of Nancy Ward and her first husband, Kingfisher. (In a battle against the Creeks, when Kingfisher was killed, Nancy Ward took over his gun and joined in, rallying the Cherokee warriors. Because of her bravery in battle, she was named Ghigau or Beloved Woman.) Cameron, to whom Corn Tassel also refers is Alexander Cameron, the British agent among them.

The beloved man who is pitched upon to hold the good talks fast with me; my beloved seats in Chote, there to hold each other forever. I had a beloved man once in my land, which was Cameron, who was always talking in my house, in behalf of the white Traders, who brought us supplies of goods. It has been but a little while dark. Here is Ellis Harland who lives in the beloved Town; when we get home, shall go to Seneca and bring us goods as usual. There is George Lowry, my Trader in Toquo, him and Colo. Gist took hold of each other, and hold the peace Talk, and friend here, knows it; I determine to send him with Ellis Harland likewise. Joseph Vann is inclined to supply us with goods; He will be living again with us verry (sic) shortly in friendship, and I hope will be agreeable to you. When I have this your warrior and my friend sitting on the seat of Justice in Chote every small thing that is heard (as often times it is from the Creek Nation) shall be sent and explained by him to my elder Brothers; and I will assist him in this good work. The Warriors that go to the great and noble Warrior, will let him know that I have this good man with me in my towns. It may be some satisfaction for him to hear, of one of Young Warriors being so well received in our beloved Town. I hope your great and noble Warrior of America, will consider my condition, because it is poor and low with me; because I think the people of South Carolina are seeking too much land from me. I hope these my friends do not take this amiss. My desire is that this powerful Warrior will give me some redress, for the great injury of taking from me one of my principal Towns.[77]

[Figure 2.0: Chief George Lowrey]

On July 19, Mr. Avery then spoke of the "everlasting doors of friendship, that shall stand open from Newbern to….Chota," and proposed what he thought would be a more agreeable boundary line.[78] He apologized for the Cherokee's mistrust of North Carolinians, but offered no exchange for their lands other than peace and friendship.

Old Tassel then arose and spoke, and refused to give up Long Island itself. His ancestors used this as an ancient and sacred treaty ground for holding talks by the "beloved fire." His great affection for his brother-in-law, Colonel Gist, was demonstrated in that he reserved it for him only, along with the Cherokees. Several accounts are given of his statements which demonstrated his adamancy concerning "the Island."

> The beloved men of Carolina shall now hear what I have to say; now I will let you know what I have to say; and I hope you'll remember, That the Island you see there belongs to Col. (sic) Gist. It is to keep the beloved fire on, to bring the Cherokees to talk by. No man shall hold any right thereto but Colo. (sic) Gist. Your beloved fire shall be on this side of the River last war your beloved fire was on this side and ours on the Island, so that it must be reserved for him.
>
> I am the man that speaks to my elder Brothers, I speak to my elder Brothers nothing but the truth as I always do. don't (sic) stop your ears, but hear and remember well. Don't forget, as people sometimes do. Observe that none are so deaf as those who will not to hear. Don't forget. Here was my elder Brother talking just now. I shall remember what was said. I shall send my great Talk to the Great Warrior of America, for him to consider what has (sic) been doing.
>
> He is the head of all, he ought to hear and consider the talks; likewise the Governor of Virginia that nothing may be hid that has been done. You have asked for the ground I walk upon; you have asked me for my land; the dividing line to begin on the River where the Virginia people left it, running thence to the Chimney top; thence across Nolachucky to the Creek

you mentioned. Let this be the line until Colo. Gist returns and brings word from the Great Warrior of America, and then the line can be marked. As you are the beloved men of Carolina, I listened to your talks they went to my heart. The land I give up will ever hold good; it will ever be as good as it is now; and when we are all dead and gone it will continue to produce. Therefore I expect when you come to run the line, that you will bring some acknowledgement. You have now come empty handed, with nothing to make us an acknowledgement for the land, which will afford bread to those yet unborn, when goods will be rotten and gone. You come here from the Governor of North Carolina to talk peace talks & make a line; but you'll tell your beloved man the value of the land. -Now I am done; I give up the land you asked; I shall say no more. If you ask for more, I will not give it. In confirmation I give you a string.

A string[79]

As though the ancients' tears fell from the heavens, knowing the sealed fate of the sacred ground and the Cherokees, a downpour of rain occurred immediately following Corn Tassel's speech, causing the commissioners, Indian chiefs and some of the warriors to retire to a house in the fort.[80]

CHAPTER 7

Col. Christian then spoke to the Cherokees on July 15, 1777. In his speech, he reminded them that if the Virginians only wanted to take their lands, they would have brought an army to their country and not have invited them to treat with them.[81]

The white people had difficulty understanding that the Cherokees thought it unclean to keep livestock and animals close to their homes, and preferred instead to keep their hunting grounds open, leaving two weeks at a time on hunting expeditions and returning with a great supply. Col. Christian proposed to give the Cherokees "two hundred head of breeding cows and one hundred head of sheep to run the boundary as proposed for the land that fell within the state of Virginia. He asserted that it was Gov. Patrick Henry and Virginia's desire to be at peace and do everything generously and justly.[82]

William Tatham transcribed as a memorandum of Corn Tassel's reply to the American Commissioners, who proposed that the Cherokees should cede a much greater extent of the country than was agreed to in the result.[83] The quality of authenticity of Corn Tassel's speeches relied upon the ability and perhaps the ability and/or willingness of the appointed interpreters to record accurately. Copies of this eloquent speech circulated and found its way into many white pioneer's cabins. William Tatham insisted that even as he transcribed, the speech lost the original native beauty.[84]

It is a little surprising that when we entered into treaties with our brothers, the whites, their whole cry is more land! Indeed, formerly it seemed to be a matter of formality with them to demand what they knew we durst not refuse.
But on the principles of fairness, of which we have received assurances during the conducting of the present treaty, and in

the name of free will and equality, I must reject your demand. Suppose, in considering the nature of your claim (and in justice to my nation I shall and will do it freely), I were to ask one of you, my brother warriors under what kind of authority, by what law, or on what pretense he makes this exorbitant demand of nearly all the lands we hold between your settlements and our towns, as the cement and consideration of peace.

Would he tell me that it is by right of conquest? No! If he did, I would retort on him that we had last marched over his territory; even up to this very place which he has fortified so far within his former limits; nay, that some of our young warriors (whom we have not yet had an opportunity to recall or give notice to, of the general treaty) are still in the woods, and continue to keep his people in fear, and that it was but till lately that these identical walls were your strongholds, out of which you durst scarcely advance.

If, therefore, a bare march, or reconnoitering a country is sufficient reason to ground a claim to it, we shall insist upon transposing the demand, and your relinquishing your settlements on the western waters and removing one hundred miles back towards the east, whither some of our warriors advanced against you in the course of last year's campaign.

Let us examine the facts of your present eruption into our country, and we shall discover your pretensions on that ground. What did you do? You marched into our territories with a superior force; our vigilance gave us no timely notice of your manouvres (sic); your numbers far exceeded us, and we fled to the stronghold of our extensive woods, there to secure our women and children.

Thus, you marched into our towns; they were left to your mercy; you killed a few scattered and defenseless individuals, spread fire and desolation wherever you pleased, and returned again to your own habitations. If you meant this, indeed, as a conquest you omitted the most essential point; you should have fortified the junction of the Holstein and Tennessee rivers, and have thereby conquered all the waters above you. But, as all are fair advantages during the existence of a state of war, it is now too late for us to suffer for your mishap of generalship!

Again, were we to inquire by what law or authority you

set up a claim, I answer, none! Your laws extend not into our country, nor ever did. You talk of the law of nature and law of nations, and they are both against you. Indeed, much has been advanced on the want of what you term *civilization* among the Indians; and many proposals have been made to us to adopt your laws, your religion, your manners and your customs. But, we confess that we do not yet see the propriety or practicability of such a reformation, and should be better pleased with beholding the good effect of these doctrines in your own practices than with hearing you talk about them, or reading your papers to us upon such subjects.

You say: Why do not the Indians till the ground and live as we do? May we not, with equal propriety, ask, Why the white people do not hunt and live as we do? You profess to think it no injustice to warn us not to kill our deer and other game from the mere love of waste; but it is very criminal in our young men if they chance to kill a cow or a hog for their sustenance when they happen to be in your lands. We wish, however, to be at peace with you, and to do as we would be done by. We do not quarrel with you for killing an occasional buffalo, bear or deer on our lands when you need one to eat; they kill all our game; our young men resent the injury, and it is followed by bloodshed and war.

This is not mere affected injury; it is a grievance which we equitably complain of and it demands a permanent redress.

The great God of Nature has placed us in different situations. It is true that he has endowed you with many superior advantages; but he has not created us to be your slaves. We are a separate people! He has given each their lands, under distinct considerations and circumstances: he has stocked yours with cows, ours with buffaloe (sic); yours with hog, ours with bear; yours with sheep, ours with deer. He has, indeed, given you an advantage in this, that your cattle are tame and domestic while ours are wild and demand not only a larger space for range, but art to hunt and kill them; they are, nevertheless, as much our property as other animals are yours, and ought not to be taken away without our consent, or for something equivalent.[85]

So attached was Corn Tassel's heritage to Long Island when it was mentioned, he requested a memorandum be attached stating: "…that the

Tassel yesterday objected against giving up the Great Island opposite to Fort Henry to any person or country whatever except Colo. Nathaniel Gist for whom and themselves it was reserved by the Cherokees...." and before placing his mark on the treaty, Tassel first reiterated:

> I told you yesterday so plain that no one could
> misunderstand, We will not dispose of this Island but we reserve
> it to hold our Great Talks on. Even the grass is for our creatures
> and the wood to kindle our beloved fire with. As Colo. Gist is
> our friend and Brother it is his ground as well as ours; and he
> may sit down and settle upon it. Then Corn Tassel hesitated
> before signing because he explained, ever since I signed a paper
> for Colo. (sic) Henderson I am afraid of signing papers. He told
> me many lies and deceived us. He never shewed to me but one
> paper and I hear he has eight or nine.[86]

To conclude the treaty, Corn Tassel expressed his willingness to represent the Cherokees, working cooperatively with North Carolina and Virginia:

> I was apprised of the matter yesterday taking hold of
> an agent. I think one is not sufficient for both States,
> I will take hold of one of the North Carolina Warriors, and take
> him home. A great number of my people at home will hear all
> the good Talks, and when I bring a warrior from each State, and
> preserve their peace and safety, then my people will see clearly.
> Now I have taken hold of my Brother from North Carolina by
> the hand. Some of my people that are ungovernable,
> may say something when I go home, but I will have the two
> beloved Warriors from both States by the hand. They can do the
> business better than one.
> As to trade and commerce, it lies in the breast of the
> seat of Government, and my two beloved men will be there to
> see that all things will be done right and taken care of. I have
> had a little trade from pensacola, (sic) things were dear. the first
> peace Talks of South Carolina and Georgia said "We see how
> your father took pity on you and supplied you with goods, but
> they were so dear you could not buy a rag to cover you (....) we
> will let you have them cheaper."

The articles of the peace treaty negotiated near the Long Island on Holston July 20, 1777 with the state of Virginia stipulated:

1. The Cherokees and whites would give mutual assistance in case of an attack by another Indian nation.
2. Any enslaved people being held by the Cherokees had to be released to an appointed agent for Virginia. Horses and cattle were to be returned.
3. Any white man who passed through the Overhill towns required having a certificate signed by the Washington County, Virginia magistrates. If the white man failed to do so, the Cherokees had the privilege of delivering him to a commanding officer at Ft. Henry or "apply to their own use" any possessions that person might have.
4. If any white man murdered an Indian, he was to be delivered to "Washington County to be tried & put to death." If any Indian murdered a white man, the Cherokees had to kill him "in the presence of the agent at Chota or two magistrates in the County of Washington."
5. As many white people as had settled below the boundary of Donaldson's Line (below the Virginia boundary and the Cherokees) "which line (was) to begin at the lower corner of Donaldson line on the north side of the River Holston and to run down that River according to the meanders thereof, and binding theron including the great Island at the mouth of Cloud's Creek,…below Warrior's ford at the mouth of Carter's Valey (sic); thence….to a high point on Cumberland mountain, between there and five miles below of westward of the great gap, which leads to the settlements of the Kentuckie (sic) this last mentioned line is to be considered the boundary between Virginia and the Cherokees. The Virginians agreed to pay a price for this land of "two hundred Cows and One hundred Sheep."
6. No white man was allowed to "settle, hunt or drive any stock below the said boundary." The articles of the treaty between the Cherokees and the state of North Carolina stipulated the same agreement except any white man who murdered an Indian would be "tryed (sic) and put to death in the nearest county." Their boundary line encompassed "all the lands to the East, East & South East of the said line."[87]

Of the boundaries, Savanooka or the Raven promised, "I shall sit at home safe....as if it was a wall that reached up to the skies."[88] North Carolina offered no monetary support to the Cherokees. Corn Tassel, while at Long Island had argued "that his people claimed the land south of Cumberland River, quite to the mouth of it." As he expected at least some exchange of goods from the Carolinians for the land, Corn Tassel disdainfully commented, "The great men of Carolina seem to hold everything very fast in their hands; they are always getting what they can and letting nothing go, neither guns, goods or ammunition."[89]

After signing the Treaty of Long Island of the Holston in 1777, Corn Tassel returned to the Overhill towns. He continued to advocate peace for the following three years, but it was an arduous charge. Alexander Cameron, the British agent among the Cherokees, explained to the chief that he could no longer supply the Overhill towns with goods unless they would reconsider their amity with the Americans. Instead, in hopes of furthering their affiliation with the British, he and Stuart bequeathed the Chickamaugans with these provisions.

Although many chiefs signed the Treaty of Long Island of 1777, the Chickamaugans had been notably absent. Open war was never declared, but both the Chickamaugans and the whites committed depredations on one another. Campbell, Sevier and Martin warned the Cherokees to make plans to meet again for a treaty at Long Island on the Holston if it was peace they truly desired.

CHAPTER 8

The purpose of this treaty meeting, held July 26, 1781 at Long Island of Holston, was to once again adjust the boundaries, to establish peace and for an exchange of prisoners. William Christian, William Preston, Arthur Campbell and Joseph Martin represented Virginia, and Evan Shelby, Joseph Williams and John Sevier represented North Carolina's interests.[90] Corn Tassel was the main speaker for the Cherokees. He discussed meetings with John McDonald, the Assistant Superintendent of Indian affairs and Walter Scott, a sub-agent, both for the British, both also traders with his people, and Colonel Thomas Brown, the British superintendent at Augusta, who succeeded Stuart. Corn Tassel addressed Colonel John Sevier as follows:

> Nay I made it bright and clear, my elder Brother need not think because I speak short that any Thing is wrong. They may believe all is Right and straight.
>
> A string
>
> There are a great many of my elder Brothers who hear me speak. I look upon your beloved men as my beloved men. I speak the Truth. A great many of you hear me. This talk is from the warriors of Chuckamogge (sic) by me they were glad when they heard the talks from Colo. Martin they desired me to inform you they would hold them fast. They recd (sic) the good Talks, and sent another. The people at Home assured me they would rest at Home, and not rise up to do Harm. That they expected to see me return Home in a short Time with the good Talks.*
>
> MacDonald & Scott joined us in our Consultations & (sic) declared it was not them who gave out the bad Talk, that has brought all the Distressed (sic) upon us; but Colo Brown, who ordered them to do it said it was good for us to come in

here to make Peace & they would write to Colo Brown we had
throwed him away and all his Talks and have no more to say to
him; having brought all the Troubles upon us. Now you are going
to hear the Talk, from all the Towns around, in the whole Nation
by me We are all joined in this talk, Providence has ordered it so,
we are all joined in this Peace; we are all joined as one man. String.

Directing himself to Col Severe (sic):

You are my elder Brother. You are a man and warrior.
I know. I have heard different talks by different people from Time
to Time quite different from what I expected. If you are angry,
I fear it was caused by some evil persons. There are now the
beloved men on both sides listening to us. You have risen up
from a warrior to a beloved man. I hope your Heart will be good
and peaceable for the Time to come, in token of my Friendship
for you I give you this String [91]
*King's People

[Figure 2.1] is Corn Tassel's speech as it was originally recorded by the
translator.]

The next day, Corn Tassel, wearing a ruffled shirt and a match coat
which had been presented to him, spoke explaining why his people had
sought revenge. He expressed hope for better times:

I am going to speak. Yesterday was a bad day. There
were many dift (sic) Talks. But all our thoughts seem good today.
I speak concerning land we are now on - it is ours. We   before
had good Talks here and where you took pity on both sides; your
people and ours. We are talking here where the beloved seats are
placed. You took pity on us before and have took pity on us a
second Time & sent for us. The good talks are begun and we hope
will be carried on. A String.

(A string of white beads were usually presented as a
symbol of the desire for peace, but in some instances,
Corn Tassel had expressed that they were presented as a reminder
for truthfulness.)

I am going to speak concerning our old Talk four years
ago. It is true a little dark cloud has been over our good Talk,
like a small flying cloud in the sky, but it has passed away. When

we had the good talks before, & took pity on both sides, you requested a small parcele (sic) of Land, which was bounded in such a manner by a high Chimney Top rock, well known to many people then present. I waited long to be sent for the Line run, but was never sent for. I look upon it as the reason I was never sent for & that the line was never run, that the People going near it would rather encroach upon our Land than run the line. I heard from Time to Time of their encroaching upon our Land and building hutts (sic) and camps upon it. When I was at Home in peace and quietness, many of my People at Times would come up the River hunting, never exheding (sic, exceeding?) the white People had gone so far down, and there meet white People hunting, who would plunder my People by taking their Horses, Guns and Kittles (sic). All this did not satisfy my older Brothers. They went to Toquo & took off ad 7000 of Horses and afterward did the same at Chota; this was the first Beginning of the last disturbance by exasperating our People—I am talking to you our elder Brother not as entering fully into the Treaty of Peace, I am letting you know what I look upon to be the Cause of the late Troubles.

Last Fall some white People brought us word that when we would be gone a hunting the White People would attack our towns & destroy our People at Home. And afterward, we received Presents & talks from the English at Augusta to go and Revenge the Thefts and Encroachments committed mourder (sic). This encouraged our people to seek Revenge and it made Things dark a while, but we hope now all will be made bright and clear again. We have now no more to say toDay (sic), we have now been letting you know what we think were the principal Cause of the late War. We will enter into the Banner of the Peace Tomorrow.[92]

In Colonel John Sevier's response to Corn Tassel, he stated, "Warriors and Chiefs, Friends and Brothers. I listened to your Talk yesterday. I listened to it with Pleasure. I own I fought with you, but it was for our own safety and not from any Delight I had in hurting you ___ I am not afraid to fight with men, but I never hurt Women & Children, They are innocent harmless things; It is true I took some of them Prisoners, but it was only with a view to exchange for our People you have as Prisoners. I have used them well, kept them at my own House and treated them as my own Children; and you shall have them everyone soon as you Bring in our People. And so will all the Carolina People, as they get acquainted with you. I am now pleased with you of your Nation. I love you. While you hope we shall love one another, with this String I bury in the ground all the Difference that has ever happened betwixt us. You may believe me, I speak from my heart."

String

[Figure 2.2: Response of Col. John Sevier as it was originally recorded.]

At this point, a Cherokee woman, Nancy Ward, the cousin of Corn Tassel, arose. She was surrounded by an accompaniment of Cherokee women. She carried a swan's wing to signify her title as Beloved Woman of the Cherokees. This was an amazing event, as it was one of the first public speeches by a woman, unheard of in white pioneer society.

Nancy Ward declared,

> You know women are always looked upon as nothing; but we are your mothers; you are our sons. Our cry is all for peace; let it continue. This peace must last forever. Let your women's sons be ours; our sons be yours. Let your women hear our words.[93]

The words of Nancy Ward seemed to evoke positive emotion on this occasion. Colonel Christian answered her speech:

> Mothers, I listen well to your Talk it is humane, soft & tender. No Man can hear it without being affected by it. Such words & thoughts from unlearned Women shows to the world that human Nature is the same in all People Learning only makes the Difference. When you (sic) Children & ours are born they are the same; and bring them up together, will still be the same. Let one of our sons be brought up amongst you & he will be like You Selves; (sic) and let one of yours be brought up well with the Heart and mind. your People are as good as ours. Mothers— Our women shall hear your word and we know will feel & think of them. We all, descended from one Woman we do not wish to quarrel with your Nation: because you are our Mothers. We will not meddle with your People if they will be still and quiet at Home, and let us live in Peace.
> 5 Strings [94]

This was one of the few treaties where land was not ceded as a result.

[Figure 2.3 shows original translation of Colonel Christian's "Mothers" speech.]

CHAPTER 9

The confusion and decline of the Cherokees coincided with the eventual death of the aged associates of Corn Tassel: Chief Attakullakulla, followed by Chief Oconistota. Alderman compared these times to a political chess game, with the Cherokees as pawns.[95] Following Oconistota's resignation due to old age and subsequent death in 1782, Corn Tassel succeeded him as principal chieftain. Because of the extreme poverty of the Cherokee towns and continued encroachments, the Overhill towns appointed Corn Tassel to a committee of chiefs to beseech the assistance of the governor of North Carolina. James Robertson, the agent among them for North Carolina, was of the opinion that if the state would supply them with goods, nothing but peace would ensue. Corn Tassel did not think it fair treatment that his people should live so poorly. Why should he have to depend upon the British for assistance? Even if the Americans had little to offer in tangible support, the Wataugans were not adhering to the treaty obligations and were illegally trespassing on Cherokee lands. How much longer could he continue to convince the Overhill people to refrain from hostilities and siding with the Chickamaugans? Many of them were already moving their families from Overhill towns to safer locations.[96]

In February of 1782, Governor Martin of North Carolina had expressed to Colonel John Sevier his distress over the complaints of the daily intrusions of our people which "are against the orders of your elder brother," and urged him "to have these intruders off" the lands.[97] Col. Sevier, being a frontiersman himself, elected to ignore this order. Surely, thought Corn Tassel, if I present the tribulations of my people to the governor, he will assist us. Therefore, with an entourage of followers, they chose their trusted "go-between": Joseph Martin, the white husband of Nancy Ward's daughter, who took Oconistota into his own home and cared for him in his dying hours. Col. Martin had, by Oconistota's request, taken the dying man back to his beloved Chota, where he buried him using a dugout canoe as a coffin. [Figure 2.6: The Grave of Oconistota in Chota, identified by the presence of the dugout canoe]

"A Talk to Colonel Joseph Martin, by the Old Tassel (the name the white pioneers called Chief Corn Tassel), in Chota, the 25th of September, 1782, in favour of the whole nation. For his excellency, the Governor of North-Carolina. Present, all the chiefs of the friendly towns and a number of young men."[98]

Brother: I am now going to speak to you. I hope you will listen to me. A string. I intended to come this fall and see you, but there was such confusion in our country, I thought it best for me to stay at home and send my Talks by our friend, Colonel Martin, who promises to deliver them safe to you. We are a poor distressed people, that is, in great trouble, and we hope our elder brother will take pity on us and do us justice. Your people from Nollichucky (sic) are daily pushing us out of our lands. We have no place to hunt on. Your people have built houses within one day's walk of our towns. We don't want to quarrel with our elder brother; we, therefore, hope our elder brother will not take our lands from us, that the Great Man above gave us. He made you and he made us; we are all his children, and we hope our elder brother will take pity on us, and not take our lands from us that our father gave us, because he is stronger than we are. We are the first people that ever lived on this land; it is ours, and why will our elder brother take it from us? It is true, sometime past, the people over the great water persuaded some of our young men to do some mischief to our elder brother, which our principal men were sorry for. But you our elder brothers come to our towns and took satisfaction, and then sent for us to come and treat with you, which we did. Then our elder brother promised to have the line run between us agreeable to the first treaty, and all that should be found over the line should be moved off. But it is not done yet. We have done nothing to offend our elder brother since the last treaty, and why should our elder brother want to quarrel with us? We have sent to the Governor of Virginia on the same subject. We hope that between you both, you will take pity on your younger brother, and send Colonel Sevier, who is a good man, to have all your people moved off our land. I should say a great deal more, but our friend, Colonel Martin, knows all our grievances, and he can inform you. A string. [99]

This disturbed Corn Tassel that no immediate response was delivered, especially when the white people continued to violate former treaties by encroaching upon the Cherokee hunting grounds. These hunting grounds were located on the "territory south-of-the French Broad-and-Holston-rivers-and-west-of-the-Big-Pigeon-River," the area later designated as "Dumplin."[100]

Adding to this chaos, depredations occurred daily committed by both races. The Chickamaugans worked to incite the Overhill towns to join them. While Corn Tassel advocated that the wisest course was to remain peaceful, the Chickamaugans of the Lower towns continued raids on the frontiers. Near Christmas of 1780, "Chota was destroyed by Alexander Campbell and John Sevier, and Chief Oconistota fled to the mountains, setting up temporary camp there.[101] In 1782, Colonel John Sevier marched against the Lower towns and destroyed everything from Bull Town on Chickamauga Creek to Estanaula, on the Coosa River. Major Fine, in 1783, destroyed the town of Cowee.

According to Williams in *Early Travels in Tennessee Country,* a minister, Brother Martin Schneider, in January of 1784, entered the Cherokee country to inquire about providing religious instruction for the Cherokees. Brother Schneider kept a diary of this experience. In comparison to his culture, he expressed that the Cherokees seemed unclean in their cooking and cleaning methods. In addition, he told of being seated around a kettle among the Cherokees and eating dried, boiled peaches with his fingers. As he left, they gave him a dozen eggs for Col. Martin, for whom he recorded, "they have great respect." He was then led to McCormick's (the interpreter's house), where about twenty Native Americans and Col. Joseph Martin (called Gulkalu, meaning "Tall") were seated. Col. Martin said he had some other business to address, but first, he told Corn Tassel that Brother Schneider was present to know if the Cherokees would like to receive religious instruction, and if a couple of missionaries could live among them for that purpose. Col. Martin assured "Taysell" (as Bro. Schneider recorded Corn Tassel's name in his journal) that they would never try to cause war, trade or take their lands.

Brother Schneider's report of his journey records, "The Head Chief said then, he would answer after some Time; & after 2 Hours he got up & said: He knew & could remember it very well that their Father (the King of England) had long ago sent once 2 Men to them as Preachers, but one of them died, & the other had not stayed long, because war had broke (sic) out in the country, which he was very sorry for. Secondly, that he believed that this man was a Wayer, that is a great man, who was sent by still greater wayers to tell them of Utajah (God) that Great Man who dwells above. Thirdly, that he was very glad that again such an offer was made to them, that they might hear & be instructed concerning him, & all the present chiefs whom he had asked about it, were of the same opinion. But he could give no positive answer, till all chiefs and hunters were at home; (the most of them were on a Beaver Hunt) but when they returned, he would call them all together to a great meeting to hear their mind, & at the next Treaty on Long Island, they would tell their Resolution."

Brother Schneider continued, explaining that Mr. McCormick, the Interpreter began to preach to the Cherokees, telling them the brethern were concerned for their soul's salvation. Mr. McCormick then promised he would do all in his power to secure the Indians' acceptance.

Brother Schneider further records the contents of a letter Col. Martin received from the Shawnees relating that they were being charged by the white people for acts of the Chickamaugans. They complained that their brethern, the Chickamaugans still continued to "lie in wait for people & steal horses, yea even at times murder people, wherewith they are charged by the white people." They expressed that they wished for peace and that it "was contrary to their custom to commit hostilities in times of peace." Col. Martin expressed that if the Chickamaugans continue, "the white people would go against them this spring."

Corn Tassel did not approve of any of the acts committed by the Chickamaugans, in fact to no avail, he tried to dissuade them. Finally, he decided the wisest course was to admit his inability to control this faction, and he turned the matter over to Colonel Martin. However, he hardly believed it when the state of North Carolina opened for settlement their Cherokee hunting grounds, which were positioned north and west of the French Broad and Tennessee rivers.

Corn Tassel received word that a Major Hubbard, who was a renowned Indian hater, shot the Chief of Citico, Gun Rod (also known as Butler), in the back. Hubbard's family had been killed by Shawnees, and he had killed more Cherokees than any white man. Corn Tassel knew that Gun Rod had resented Hubbard, once being unhorsed by this man in an earlier encounter. To the Cherokee, it was the ultimate act of humiliation to be unhorsed by someone. As it was reported by Hubbard, Gun Rod, "panting for an opportunity to retrieve his loss," fired at Hubbard, the ball passing between his ear and head, actually cutting the hair. Apparently, the Cherokee reported the incident differently, as Governor Martin received information from the Native Americans that "a daring murder had been committed....without provocation."[102] Corn Tassel had no premonition that he, the peace keeper, would someday face Major Hubbard as a result of postulatory avengement. Following this incident, Governor Josiah Martin, governor of the North Carolina, sent Samuel Henderson, giving instruction and full license to find out to what extent injuries were inflicted on the Cherokees and the unfairness of the western white pioneers. The governor also forwarded, by Major Henderson, a talk from himself to the Cherokees, and a letter to General John Sevier. Given are these correspondences:

TO THE OLD TASSEL AND OTHER WARRIORS OF
THE CHEROKEE NATION:
Brothers: I have received your talk by Colonel Martin, in behalf
of yourself and all the Cherokee nation. I am sorry that you
have been uneasy, and that I could not see you this last spring,
as I promised you, as our beloved men met at Hillsbourough
(sic) had prevented me, by agreeing and concluding among
themselves, that the Great Council of the thirteen American
States, at Philadelphia, should transact all affairs belonging to the
Red People.
        (The "Great Council" to which Governor Martin referred
was from May 25 to September 17, 1787, and is now what we call
the "Constitutional Convention.")
        The correspondence included the following:
        Brother: It gives me great uneasiness that our people
trespass on your lands, and that your young men are afraid to
go a-hunting on account of our people ranging the
woods and marking the trees. These things, I can assure you, are
against the orders of your elder brother, and are not approved
by me and the good men of North-Carolina; but while we were
consulting our council of Philadelphia, our bad men living near
your lands thought we had laid aside all government over them,
and that they had a right to do as they pleased; and not willing
to obey any law for the sake of ill gain and profit, care not what
mischief they do between the red and white people, if they can

enrich themselves. But, brother, I know your complaints and will endeavour (sic) to set your minds at ease, by ordering off all these persons from your lands, who have settled on them without your consent. Your friend, Gen. Sevier, is made our First Warrior for the western country, to whom Colonel Martin carries my particular directions to have these intruders moved off. About the 25th, of April, I propose to meet you, and such of your beloved men as will be pleased to attend, at the Great Island in Holston, or other place most agreeable to you on Broad or that river. I shall bring with me some of our first men, who will assist in the Talks, in whom, as well as myself, you can place your confidence and trust. I propose to bring with me the goods, which, in my last Talk, I informed you, were intended to purchase your right and claim to some of the lands near you, that a line be drawn and marked between your people and ours, which shall be the bounds in future, and over which our people shall not go and settle upon, without being highly punished.

Brother: In the meanwhile, I beg you not to listen to any bad Talks, which may be made by either white or red people, which may disturb our peace and good will to each other; and should mischief be done by any of our bad people, be patient until you hear from me, and may be certain your elder brother of North-Carolina will do everything in his power, to give your minds satisfaction. I am told the northern Indians have sent you some bad Talks, but do not hear them, as they wish to make variance between all the red and American people without any provocation.

Brother: Colonel Martin, your friend, has told me your grievances. I wish to redress them as soon as possible. I cannot come to you sooner than I have proposed. Bad men may make you uneasy, but your elder brother of North Carolina has you greatly in his heart, and wishes to make you sensible of it.[103]

GOVERNOR MARTIN
TO GENERAL SEVIER: DANBURY, December,1784
Sir: By Major Outlaw, I sent your brigadier's commission, which I expect you have received, and which I hope will be acceptable to you, as also some proclamations agreeably to a request of the Legislature, to have all the intruders removed off the Indian

lands. I request your attention, to this business, as I have received a Talk from the Cherokee nation, greatly complaining of trespasses daily committing against them; and their young men are afraid to hunt, as our people are continually ranging their woods and marking their trees. The importance of keeping peace with the Indians you are sufficiently impressed with, and the powers with which you are armed, are sufficient to check the licentious and disobedient, and remove every impediment out of the way, which may give the Indians uneasiness.

I am informed a daring murder has been committed, on one Butler [Gun Rod], a Cherokee Indian, by Major Hubbard, of Greene county (sic), without any provocation. I have given directions for his being apprehended and conveyed to Burke Gaol for security, until the setting of Washington Superior Court, when he will be remanded back. Col. Gist, of Greene county (sic), is entrusted with this service. I have directed him to call on you for guards if the same be necessary. You will please to write to me the first opportunity on this subject. I propose to hold a treaty with the Indians about the 25th of April, at the Great Island. Governor Caswell and Colonel Blount will be commissioners to assist at the treaty, where I shall expect you to attend with such guard as will be thought necessary, and of which you will hereafter have advice.[104]

Meanwhile, the State of Franklin and John Sevier, governor of this proposed state to be admitted as the fourteenth state, emerged totally in sympathy with the white pioneers. Therefore, no restraints were placed upon their invasions. One of the State of Franklin's first legislative acts was to hold a treaty with the Cherokees at Dumplin Creek. This treaty was held May 31, 1785, without Corn Tassel and the other head men present, as they refused to attend.

Once again, Corn Tassel desperately wrote the governors of North Carolina and Virginia, with James McCormack interpreting,

CHOTA, 19TH SEPTEMBER, 1785

Brother: I am now going to speak to you; I hope you will hear me.

I am an old man, and almost thrown away by my elder brother. The ground I stand on is very slippery, though I still hope my elder brother will hear me and take pity on me, as we were all made by the same Great Being above; we are all children of the same parent. I therefore hope my elder brother will hear me.

You have often promised me, in Talks that you sent me, that you would do me justice, and that all disorderly people should be moved off our lands; but the longer we want to see it done, the farther it seems off. Your people have built houses in sight of our towns. We don't want to quarrel with you, our elder brother; I therefore beg that you, our elder brother, will have your disorderly people taken off our lands immediately, as their being on our grounds causes great uneasiness. We are very uneasy, on account of a report that is among the white people that all themselves a new people, that lives on French Broad and Nolechuckey (sic); they say they have treated with us for all the lands on Little River. I now send this to let my elder brother know how it is. Some of them gathered on French Broad, and sent for us to come and treat with them; but as I was told there was a treaty to be held with us, by orders of the great men of the thirteen states, we did not go to meet them, but some of our young men went to see what they wanted. They first wanted the land on Little River. Our young men told them that all their head men were at home; that they had no authority to treat about lands. They then asked them liberty for those that were then living on the lands, to remain there, till the head men of their nation were consulted on it, which our young men agreed to. Since then, we are told that they claim all the lands on the waters of Little River, and have appointed men among themselves to settle their disputes on our lands, and call it their ground. But we hope you, our older brother, will not agree to it, but will have them moved off. I also beg that you will send letters to the Great Council of America, and let them know how it is; that if you have no power to move them off, they have, and I hope they will do it.

I once more beg that our elder brother will take pity on us, and not take our ground from us, because he is stronger than we. The Great Being above, that made us all, placed us on this land, and gave it to us, and it is ours. Our elder brother, in all the treaties we ever had, gave it to us also, and we hope he will not think of taking it from us now.

I have sent with this Talk a string of white beads, which I

hope my elder brother will take hold of, and think of his younger brother, who is now in trouble, and looking to him for justice. Given out by the Old Tassel, for himself and whole nation, in presence of head men of the Upper and Lower Cherokees, and interpreted by me.

JAMES McCORMACK[105]

Indeed, the State of Franklin had established a government of its own. Behaving toward the Cherokee outside of any established laws, they were illegal, and Corn Tassel, an intelligent man, recognized this. When Governor Martin heard of this independent government, he wrote to the newly appointed Governor Sevier:

> Sir: With some concern, I have heard that the counties of Washington, Sullivan and Greene, have lately declared themselves independent of the State of North-Carolina, and have chosen you governor—that you have accepted the same, and are now acting with a number of officers under the authority of a new government....

Then he added,

> ....You will also please inform me respecting the late Proclamations to remove off all intruders on Indian lands, and what is done in Hubbard's case, of which I wrote you by Colonel Martin.

Governor Martin then sent another talk addressed: "To the Old Tassel of Chota, and all the warriors of the Friendly Towns of the Cherokee nation:"

> Brothers: The time is about arriving when I expected to have held a great Talk with you, as I promised by Col. Martin, and hope you will not charge me with being false and faithless to my promise, when I explain to you the reason why this business is obliged to be put off to some longer time. I am sorry to give you this information, as the fault is not yours or mine; but, from a circumstance I could not have foreseen, would have happened, while we were preparing to see each other to exchange

mutual pledges of lasting friendship. A String.

Our brothers, the white people between the mountains and you, wish to have a council of beloved men and government separate from your elder brothers of North-Carolina, with whom they heretofore sat and held all their councils in common.

Your elder brothers are not yet agreed to their separation from them, till they are a more numerous and stronger people, till we have held Talks together on the terms of the separation, and till the great Council at New-York are agreed; while these things are settling among ourselves, the talking with you must be delayed, as the meeting must be on the ground where they live, and from whom we must procure things necessary for the support of you and us; and by this Talk we intend to make a chain of friendship strong and bright, that will last forever between you and all your elder brothers, more especially those who live near you. We wish to have their full consent and hearty assistance as one people in this business. A String.

Brothers: Be not discouraged at this delay. Whatever disputes may be between your elder brothers, I trust will not concern you, more than you may think the time long we may take up in understanding ourselves. In the meantime, I, as your elder brother, request you to be peaceably disposed to all the white people who are our brothers, and not suffer any mischief to be done to them, either to their persons or property, nor listen to any ill Talks which may be offered you, either from the red or white bad people; but should any injury be done you by the white people near you, complain to their head and beloved men, who I hope will give you redress, till the way is clear for you and us of North-Carolina to see each other. A String.

Brothers: The time is shortly to be, by the nature of our government, when I am to become a private brother, but the good Talks that have passed between us will not be forgotten. I will deliver them carefully to my successor, Governor Caswell, who loves you, and wishes to Talk with you in the same manner I have. He will have the conducting of the future Talks with you, which I hope will always be to our mutual satisfaction.[106]

Moore sums up the perspective of both races as he states "… when that government fell, and all support was withdrawn from them, they boldly erected for themselves an independent government in the midst of the Cherokee reservation. The history of American colonization does not exhibit a more daring, heroic, and alas! lawless struggle for the possession of a country than that waged by the pioneers of Dumplin.... On the other hand, the Indians who opposed these aggressive masterful backwoodsmen appeal not less strongly to our sympathy....their feeling of utter helplessness in the presence of great wrongs; the impotent chafing of their proud spirits as they saw their hunting grounds diminish, and the wild game grow scarcer, rendered their position pathetic in the Extreme."[107]

CHAPTER 10

Corn Tassel, then known by the name, Koatohee, travelled to South Carolina in the fall of 1785, accompanied by Scollacutta or Hanging Maw. Among the nearly one thousand Cherokees who went were chiefs of the various towns, with picturesque English interpreted names such as: Prince, Rising Fawn, Young Terrapin, Buffalo White Calf, the Rabbit, Yellow Bird, Sour Mush, Porpoise and the Cabin.[108] The Hopewell Treaty was held on Andrew Pickens' plantation.[109]

The plantation was located on the Keowee River in the town of Hopewell, South Carolina.[110] Besides Pickens, the other commissioners were Lachlan McIntosh, Joseph Martin and Benjamin Hawkins, Commissioners of the United States.[111] This was the first treaty between the United States and the Cherokees.[112]

The commissioners agreed with the Cherokees in this treaty to dissolve terms of all previous treaties, such as Dumplin Creek, and restored much of the disputed lands. These commissioners were men whom the Cherokees believed honored fair treatment in regulating the western boundaries of white settlers and establishing peaceful relations. Emmett Starr's *History of the Cherokees* recorded that,"Bob" Benge, grandnephew of Corn Tassel, named one of his sons "Pickens" Benge. Whether the choice had a connection to Andrew Pickens is unknown.

One of the commissioners explained, "Congress is now sovereign of all of our country, which we point out for you on the map. They want none of your lands, or anything else which belongs to you. As an earnest of their regard for you, we propose to enter into a treaty perfectly equal and conformable to what we now tell you. If you have any grievances, we will hear them, and will take such measures to correct them as may be proper.[113]

Standing under a huge spreading oak, thereafter always known as the "Treaty Oak," Corn Tassel responded of this,

The land we are now on is the land we were fighting
for in the late war. The Great Man above made it for us to subsist
upon. The red men are the aborigines of this country. It is but
a few years since the white men found it. I am of the first stock,
a native of this land. The white people are now living upon
it as our friends. From the beginning of the friendship between
white people and red, beads have been given as confirmation of
friendship, as I now give you these beads.

(A string)

....The people of North Carolina have taken our lands without
consideration, and are now making their fortunes out of them.[114]

Corn Tassel, with his dark and aging hand, accepted a map
from the commissioners. On it, he slowly and carefully marked where
the boundary locations of the claimed Cherokee territory. As he pointed
out on the map to the commissioners, he had hope that he finally had a
receptive audience and now was the time to deliver his grievances toward
the white settlers. He continued,

In the forks of French Broad and Holston are three thousand white
people on our lands. This is a favored spot, and we cannot give it up. It is
within twenty-five miles of our towns. These people must be removed.[115]

The commissioners, realizing that what Corn Tassel asked of
them could not be accomplished without a war against their own people,
responded that the white settlers "were too numerous, and cannot be
removed. They settled here when the Cherokees were under protection
of the King of England. you (sic) should have asked the King to remove
them." Corn Tassel challenged them with his reply,

Is not Congress, which conquered the King of England,
strong enough to remove these people?[116]

Taking a considerable amount of time to pause and reflect as if
studying the map carefully, Corn Tassel wondered why the commissioners
insisted upon even honoring the boundaries established with the British.

The aged Corn Tassel continued,

The Cherokees once owned all of this land. It is but a few years
since the white men came. We are willing for the white men to
live here as our friends, but some have over-run our boundaries.

They requested a little land and then took much. Attakullakulla and Oconostato are dead. The treaties they signed did not suit all of us.[117]

The commissioners commented,

You know, Old Tassel, that Colonel Henderson, Oconostota and the Little Carpenter are all dead," to which the orator and Beloved Man of his people replied,

I know they are dead, and I am sorry for it, and I suppose it is now too late to recover it. If Henderson were living, I should have the pleasure of telling him he was a liar. We will begin at Cumberland, and say nothing more about Kentucky, although it is justly ours. In the forks of French Broad and Holston, there are three thousand white people on our lands. That is a favored spot, and we cannot give it up. Is not Congress, which conquered the King of England strong enough to remove these people?[118]

The speeches continued with various Cherokee speakers which alternated with the words of the white men. Corn Tassel passed a string of white beads to signify his wish for peace and called upon Nancy Ward to come forward and speak. Corn Tassel realized by now the great effect Nancy Ward's words had on influencing the white settlers at the previous treaty. In the Cherokee society, a woman's opinion was highly valued, and particularly that of their Beloved Woman.

She stood in a distinguished manner with her dark handsome face erect, displaying a prominent nose, as she bravely asserted to this audience of Cherokees and white pioneers, who were both enveloped by the shadow of the oak tree.

I am glad there is now peace. I take you by hand in real friendship. I have a pipe and a little tobacco to give to the commissioners to smoke in friendship. I look on you and the red people as my children....You having determined on peace is most pleasant to me for I have seen much trouble during the late war. I am old, but I hope yet to bear children, who will grow up and people our Nation, as we are now under the protection of Congress and shall have no more disturbance. The talk I have given you is from the young warriors I have raised in my town, as well as myself. They rejoice that we have peace, and hope the chain of friendship will never more be broken.[119] Nancy Ward delivered two strings of wampum, a pipe, and some tobacco to the white commissioners.[120]

After ten days of negotiations, the articles of the Hopewell Treaty concluded on November 28, 1785, and stipulated that the boundaries determined at the Treaty of Long Island of the Holston were those by which the white settlers must abide. The "Treaty" of Dumplin was dissolved. Much to the Chickamaugans' delight, the treaty stipulated that if any citizen of the United States settled within the established domain, they would forfeit the right to be protected by the United States government, and the Cherokee had the right as deemed appropriate to punish them.[121]

The commissioners for the first time appeared to have some understanding of the Cherokee society involving war, requesting that the old Cherokee laws of retaliation be abolished, and "that the hatchet be buried." It was not that the Chickamaugans were bloodthirsty savages, but that the white men would encroach was predeterminable based upon their past together. The commissioners had actually given them license to have war. In their mind's eyes, Bob Benge and Dragging Canoe began to sharpen the war hatchets.

While the Cherokees gained some of their territory, they lost practically all of upper South Carolina, certain parts of Georgia, North Carolina and Tennessee to the white men. They had argued over lands which the Cherokees complained were settled before their permission was requested, while the commissioners from other states were angered to relinquish lands which in their opinion the Cherokees had ceded. The latter was an especially heated topic, as these lands had been set aside as bounty lands for war veterans of the Revolution.[122]

There were nine hundred and eighteen Cherokees who attended the treaty. The commissioners, thinking that only the chiefs would attend were embarrassed that they had only brought a small amount of presents to distribute.[123]

The terms of the treaty asked the Cherokees to restore prisoners and property and the whites would do likewise. Boundaries were defined and no U. S. citizen was to settle on Indian lands, or the Cherokees could punish them. The U. S. offered protection to the Cherokees. The Cherokees were to deliver any criminals who committed robbery, murder or capital crimes. Crimes against the Cherokee by a citizen of the U. S. would be punished.

In addition, the U. S. stipulated that they would regulate trade. The Cherokees were required to advise if there were any known designs agains the U. S. by other tribes or people. They also invited the Cherokees to send a representative to Congress, and further advised peace and friendship was ongoing.

Unfortunately, Nancy Ward, Corn Tassel and the other chiefs did not realize that the Confederation Congress would not be able to prevent the Watauga settlers's advancement. Falsely secure that he was backed by Congress, Scollacutta or Hanging Maw even took the compasses of some pioneer surveyors, which the Cherokees called "land stealers," and smashed them against a tree. This, nor any demands of Congress stopped the frontiersman.[124] In fact, other than public announcement, Congress did nothing to physically restrain or prevent the encroachment.

CHAPTER 11

As could be predicted, the land north of the Little Tennessee River opened for white settlement. Too close for Corn Tassel's comfort, the white pioneer settled along the banks of the opposite shore. Now, only the Little Tennessee River divided them from the Overhill Cherokees.

The Chickamaugans of the Lower towns were infuriated and killed whites frequently. Corn Tassel made visits to their towns to plead with them to cease their hostilities, but although they received the elderly man with the utmost kindness and respect, the Chickamaugans continued to "march to the beat of a different drummer." Finding them impossible to dissuade, and having no alternative, Corn Tassel advised Indian agent Joseph Martin of his disapproval of the depredations and of his inability to control or take responsibility for the Chickamaugans as a part of his people. Ironically, many of them were his own relatives: brothers, nephews and grand nephews. Finally, he turned the matter over to agent Martin.

In 1782, Colonel Sevier marched against the Lower towns and destroyed everything from Bull Town to Chickamauga Creek to Estanaula, on the Coosa River. In 1783, Major Fine destroyed Cowee, on the headwaters of the Little Tennessee. In 1786, Governor John Sevier of Franklin, crossed the Unaka Mountain and destroyed the Valley towns, on the Hiwassee River.[125] These campaigns were directed at the Chickamaugans, but ignored that Corn Tassel and the Overhills were a separate faction. Within a year of the Treaty of Dumplin, the white people passed the line established by it. Because an old warrior from Chickamauga hired a man to avenge the recent death of his sons at the hands of the whites, the Franklin authorities announced to the other chiefs that they intended to take these lands, which they had passed over, lying north of the Tennessee River. Colonels Alexander Outlaw and William Cocke at the head of two hundred and fifty militiamen, marched to Chota Ford and sent for the head men of the towns.[126] When Corn Tassel and Hanging Maw came forward, they charged them with murdering the men.

All of the following talks were a forced treaty "on the spot" between two colonels from the State of Franklin and Chiefs Corn Tassel and Hanging Maw. This set of demands upon the Cherokees was named the Treaty of Coyatee, and it took place on July 31 and August 3, 1786. Corn Tassel responded,

> Now I am going to speak to you, brothers. We have smoked. The Great Man above sent the tobacco. It will make your hearts straight. I come from Chota. I see you. You are my brothers. I see what it has done is the cause of you coming. I am glad to see my brothers and hold them fast by the hand. The Great Man made us both, and he hears the Talk. The Great Man stopped you here to hear my Talk. They are not my people that spilt the blood and spoiled the good Talk a little. My town is not so; they will always use you well whenever they see you. The men that did the murder are bad men and no warriors. They are gone. They lived at Coytoy (sic, meaning Coyatee) at the mouth of the Holston. This is all I have to say. They have done the murder. Now I give you good talk. I will tell you about the land; what you say concerning the land, I will talk to Congress about, and the man that sold it I shall look to for it. You say that North Carolina sold you the land over the river. We will talk to all our Head men about it. The Great Man above has sent you this white Talk to straight your hearts through. I give you this pipe in token of a straight Talk. I am very sorry my people has (sic) done wrong to occasion you to turn your backs. A little talk is as good as much talk; too much is not good.[127]

These Indigenous men at Coyatee, against the general advisement in council of Corn Tassel, ventured out on their own. They knew that the Treaty of Hopewell stipulated that they could kill trespassers at will, and they thought it ridiculous advice not to carry it out.

The commissioners spoke directly and gave the following ultimatum to Corn Tassel:

> We now....talk plain and straight....that North Carolina has sold us all of the country on the north side of the Tennessee [Little Tennessee] and the Holston; that we intend to settle on it, and....

if you kill any of our people for settling there, we shall destroy the town that does the mischief.[128]

Colonels Alexander Outlaw and William Cocke with their forces went to Coyatee and professed to have killed the two Indians who actually committed the act. Outlaw and Cocke felt justified in their avengement, even though these acts would have been illegal under the terms of the Hopewell Treaty. Then they returned to Chota Ford and requested again to confer with Corn Tassel and Hanging Maw. Here they made the outrageous accusation that the chiefs themselves had murdered Colonels Donelson and Christian[129] Furthermore, for the act of the men at Coyatee killing the encroachers, they demanded of Corn Tassel that they surrender all of the remaining land north of the Little Tennessee.

Corn Tassel calmly invited the men to smoke and being familiar with the Cherokee way, they submitted. Tassel held his tobacco pouch which had been carefully embroidered by his wife, and removed from it a stone pipe decorated with bits of dangling deer hair. He gave a short talk, noticing that although they were willing to smoke, they were extremely impatient with his words. Corn Tassel had never heard of this purchase of land, even though he had attended the treaty of Hopewell with the members of Congress the previous fall. Despite what Colonels Alexander Outlaw and William Cocke claimed, they had never purchased the land of which they spoke.

Corn Tassel in the following speech states that it was news to him that they had purchased it, but since he was powerless to change matters, he hoped they could live on the land peacefully.

Corn Tassel, having no better recourse, signed the treaty.
Brothers:-You have spoke (sic) to me. I am very thankful to you
for it. My brother, William Christian, took care of every body
(sic), and was a good man; he is dead and gone. It was not
me nor my people that killed him. They told lies on me. I loved
Col. Christian, and he loved me. He was killed going the other
way, over the big river. I never heard of your Great Council
giving you the land you speak of. I talked last fall with the great
men of Congress, but they told me nothing of this. I remember
that the great men and I talked together last fall and did not
think this murder would have happened so soon. We
talk good together now, but the great people, a good way off,

don't talk so good as you; they have spoke (sic) nothing to us about the land, but now you have told us the truth. We hope we shall live friends together on it, and keep our young men at peace as we all agree to sign the above terms and live brothers here after.

Wm. Cocke	his
Alex. Outlaw	Old X Tassel
Saml. Wear	mark
Henry Conway	his
Thomas Ingles	Hanging X Maw
Attest-Joseph Conway	mark[130]

This was the "Treaty " of Coyatee.

CHAPTER 12

Corn Tassel received a letter from Governor Randolph of Virginia, the contents of which he did not appreciate. Responding to it, Corn Tassel disclaimed the rumor that there had been a woman burned at Chickamauga and that no one had been burned in his nation since the Treaty of Long Island ten years ago. Owing to Corn Tassel's reputation, it was "no doubt truthfully."[131] He reminded the governor that when they fixed the boundaries they were to last "as long as the Sun shined or water Run."[132] By now, Corn Tassel did not need to attend a treaty to know every time one was held or a boundary was fixed, the "people settle(d) much faster shortly after a Treaty than Before." In fact, Corn Tassel's most famous line often quoted in early Tennessee histories was contained in this letter. It summarized the relationship between the white pioneers and the Cherokees of the eighteenth century. "Truth is," he said, "if we had no Land (sic) we should have Fewer Enemies."

Corn Tassel, a man with the ability to learn from past experience, was weary of being the constant negotiator in a situation with little likelihood of being resolved fairly. He reprimanded the governor for his patronization of the Cherokees. Corn Tassel was beginning to sympathize more with the Chickamaugans when he stated, "Great part of our Ill treatment has proceeded from me in keeping my young men from Doing mischief.

The full proceeds of the letter are as follows:

June 28, 1787—A Talk Delivered by the old Corn Tassel, a Cherokee Chief, for the Governor of Virginia, in Chota, ye 12th of June, 1787:

Brother: I this Day Received your talk open without any Date or Direction, which I think Very strange of, as I have had many From the Beloved men of Virginia, which was always sealed and Directed, (sic) as was very good. But your Letter I Don't like. It says too much about fire and sword, and accuses us of things we are clear of-in particular Burning a woman in Chickamogga (sic), which is not true. There has never been any person Burnt in our nation since the first Treaty at Long Island,   which is ten years Past. It seems as if you was (sic) fond of Beleiving (sic) Lies and Looking over Truth. We have had several Letters from the Beloved men of Virginia, which was all Good. When peace was made you was (sic) not Governor, and the first letter you ever sent it was fire and sword, and charge us with things we are clear of. If you are a Just man you will Enquire into matters Before you write so Rash, and stand to the Truth. I remember very well, and so may you, that your Beloved men appointed Commissioners promised in the name of Virginia that the Bounds then fixt (sic), on should stand as long as the Sun shined or water Run. All this, I suppose is forgot (sic) by you, Because (sic) it is true your people has (sic) settled to our Towns; tho' (sic) you say nothing about that, tho' (sic) the faith of your Country is at stake on it; but if any Person tells you any thing (sic) that is bad about us you can believe that and threaten us with fire and sword.

It is well known that I have done everything in my power to keep peace in my land and hold fast all the treaties and Good Talks and keep my young men from doing mischief, and I wish I had no greater cause to complain than you have. I observe in every treaty that we have had that a bound is fixt (sic), but we always find that your people settle much faster shortly after a Treaty than Before. It is well known that you have taken almost all our Country from us without our consent. That Don't (sic) seem to satisfy my Elder Brother, but he still talks of fire and sword. I suppose some person Has told my Elder Brother this in order to have us Drove off, as they may Take what Little Land we have left, which is very Little, not sufficient to keep us much Longer from Perishing. Truth is, if we had no Land (sic) we should have Fewer Enemies. I hope my Elder Brother will be more serious, and consider Before he writes so Rash, and Enquire whether his people or mine are most in fault. I make no Doubt but you are a great man, and suppose we are a foolish people; but we have seen enough to know we are Used Ill. Great part of our Ill treatment has proceeded from me in keeping my young men from Doing mischief. Had I suffered them to kill people when they should find them hunting and settling our land Like the Creeks and Shonies (sic, meaning Shawnees), I suppose they would not settl'd (sic) so much of our country, but I would not suffer them to hurt any white man Trusting to the fair promises of my Elder Brother, that he would Remove his people of my land; but instead of that, he wants fire and sword, without taking any notice of his people's Encroaching and Ill treatment. I am Desirous of living in peace with my Elder Brother of Virginia, and shall continue to keep good order in my Towns Till (sic) I hear further from my elder Brother, which I hope will be very soon.

Corn Tassle (sic)[133]

With treaties being forced upon them, and land disappearing like a rug pulled out from under their feet, many of the Cherokees were like caged angry wildcats in their scorching desire for retaliation. Corn Tassel continued to remind them that they "may kill a great many of them, even four, five, or six thousand and as many more will come in their place."[134] However, he was at the same time convinced that his people were drowning in the flood of emigration.

In a desperate attempt, he decided to make a journey to Philadelphia. He wondered if Congress was even aware of what was happening to his people. To be pursuing what would seem a lengthy, toilsome expedition, for this timeworn elder, only illustrated his character of heroic will. He knew in his heart it may be the final recourse in preserving the Cherokee as a people, much less their lands.

Corn Tassel visited Philadelphia in 1787, for the purpose of laying before Congress, the complaints of his people against the whites because of trespasses on the domain of the Cherokees. He met with Benjamin Franklin after his arduous trek, who related that Congress was not in session at this time, with words he thought an Indian might understand:

"I am sorry that the Great Council Fire of our Nation is not now burning, so that you cannot do your business there. In a few months the coals will be raked out of the ashes, and the fire will again be kindled. Our wise men will then take the complaints and desires of your Nation into consideration and take proper measures for giving you satisfaction (June 30, 1787)."[135]

Corn Tassel witnessed on this journey the numbers of white people, the great army, and powerful structures the Americans possessed. It was as his trustworthy contemporaries professed. If only he could have spoken and possessed the hearts of the Great Warriors of America with his gift of diplomacy and sincere desire for their decency. Corn Tassel packed away the unsmoked peace pipe and the many strings of white beads. He had rehearsed countless speeches along the trails as he lagged behind his loyal braves, shared only with the Great Spirit above. It was a regrettable journey and a long path to the shaky existence in the Cherokee homeland.

In the meantime, the State of Franklin collapsed and their former governor, John Sevier, was on the run, not holding any office, civil or military. A "fugitive on the frontiers," he accompanied Gun Rod's assassin, Major James Hubbard, and a small body of mounted riflemen.[136]

Word travelled to Chiefs Corn Tassel and Old Abram that John Sevier had entered the Overhill Country. Worried that he might bring injury to people of the Overhill area, Corn Tassel and Old Abram hastily went to meet him to make him assured of their peaceful intentions. Old Abram, like Corn Tassel, was a friendly Cherokee. He declared publicly "that if the Indians went to war, he would remain at his own house, and would never quit it."[137]

A white pioneer by the name of John Kirk built a cabin twelve miles south of Knoxville, which enraged some Cherokee warriors from Chilhowie. The Kirks did not move to the protection of the fort, as many other families did in 1788 in response to warnings by Sevier and Hubbard. Mr. Kirk and his son were away from the house when a Cherokee named Slim Tom, who was known to this family, led a party of warriors to the cabin, and killed eleven of the family members. Not long afterward, the son, John Kirk, Jr., came home and found his dead family, sounded the alarm, and several hundred militia members assembled under John Sevier.[138]

This party of John Sevier went up the Tennessee to the towns along it, killed several Cherokees and burned their towns. Old Abram lived with his son on the north side of the Tennessee. Hubbard's troops split from Sevier's and "destroyed the town of Chilhowie to punish those Indians for the Kirk massacre, Slim Tom....being from that place."[139] Hubbard sent for Old Abram to come over the river and meet the troops. Once they came, he directed them to bring Corn Tassel and Hanging Maw, that he might hold peace talks with them. He raised a truce flag to signify his peaceful intent. Corn Tassel saw the welcome flag as a sign of hope, and anxiously responded. Carrying his own white flag, he cheerfully waved it as he met the troops, ready to arrange terms of peace. Major Hubbard then invited them to his headquarters, "Sevier being absent for some time on the business of his command."[140]

As soon as the chiefs and their sons were within his lines, Hubbard had them conveyed to a vacant house in the Overhill town of Chilhowie.[141] Corn Tassel was confused by this move, but "readily complied" hoping a series of great talks and pipe smoking would make their hearts straight and good. The Cherokee men sat awaiting Hubbard and the other white men, who seemed to be loitering outside of the cabin and peering suspiciously in the windows. Major Hubbard then walked in escorting young Kirk, whose family was recently killed by a "marauding band of Cherokees."[142] He placed in John Kirk, Jr.'s hand a tomahawk and said, "Take the vengeance to which you are entitled."[143] He turned Kirk loose with a tomahawk where the now white haired and aged Corn Tassel and the others sat enclosed, the white people on the outside of the house as spectators as Major Hubbard guarded the door.

Corn Tassel, who then understood and accepted his fate, immediately "cast his countenance and eyes to the ground, "met the final blow upon his head "with fortitude" and fell dead at Kirk's feet.[144] The others, "taking their cue from (Corn Tassel) offered no resistance and were slaughtered one at a time, unarmed, peaceful, and under a flag of truce."[145]

CHAPTER 13

Legend had it among the Cherokees that "subsequently, the invaders having withdrawn, the (Cherokee) people returned. Carrion birds had devoured the body of one chief; but that of Kahn' yah' tah' hee[146] (Corn Tassel), the Beloved of all, was untouched and unchanged, even in death. His hand still grasped the violated Flag of Peace, and upon his dead life lingered a benignant smile."[147]

John Haywood, noted as "Father of Tennessee History" (1753-1826) gave his own interpretation of this untimely event:

> It is much to be regretted that history, in the pursuit of truth, is obliged to record, to the shame and confusion of ourselves, a deed of such superlative atrocity, perfidy, cowardice, and inhumanity. Surely something is due to wounded feelings, and some allowance is to be made for the conduct of men acting under the smart of great and recent suffering. But never should it be forgotten by an American soldier that his honor must be unspotted; that a noble generosity must be the regulator of his actions; that inviolable fidelity in all that is promised an enemy is a duty of sacred obligation; and that a beneficent and delicate behavior to his captive is the brightest ornament of his character.[148]

Brown added in Old Frontiers, "No more shameful deed is recorded in American history," and quotes The North Carolina State Records 22:697, "Kirk told Sevier that if he had suffered at the hands of the Indians as had the Kirk family, Sevier would have acted the same as he, himself had."[149]

General Andrew Pickens of the Hopewell Treaty, seethed at this injustice, while the Continental Congress found it reprehensive. When Governor Johnston, of North Carolina received the news of Corn Tassel's death, he issued John Sevier a warrant charging him with treason. Governor Johnston said regarding Sevier, "I fear that we shall have no peace in the western counties until this robber and free booter is checked."[150] General Joseph Martin, with hostile feelings toward Sevier, had written Governor Johnston a letter of complaint in which he "spoke of Sevier in terms of severe reprehension."[151]

John Tipton, in a brutal manner did handcuff and arrest John Sevier, and sent him to Morgantown, North Carolina. Tradition has it, that one of the guards had orders to kill Sevier on the way. However, once Sevier reached Morganton, he was among old comrades who fought with him at the Battle of King's Mountain.[152] He was released "in open daylight" and went home "with his friends."[153]

A disastrous outcome for the white pioneers took place at Gillespie's Station. The Chickamaugans led a successful attack. Joseph Martin was practically forced into position he didn't want, in going against the Chickamaugans. Many of his men deserted him because of his affinity with the Cherokees. A letter was left by the Cherokees dated October 15, 1788 and addressed as follows:

> To Mr. John Sevier and Joseph Martin, and to You, the Inhabitants of the New State
>
> We wish to inform you of the accident that happened at Gillespie's Fort, concerning the women and children that were killed in the battle. "The Bloody Fellow's" talk is that he is now upon his own ground. He is not like you are; for you kill women and children, and he does not. He had orders to do it, and to order them off the land; and he came and ordered them to surrender, and that they should not be hurt; and they would not, and he stormed and took it. For you beguiled the head man (referring to Chief Corn Tassel), that was your friend and wanted to keep peace; but you began it, and this is what you get for it. When you move off the land, then we will make peace and give up the women and children; and you must march off in thirty days. Five thousand is our number.
>
> Bloody Fellow
> Categisky
> John Watts
> Glass[154]

In 1791, Hubbard led a party of sixteen men down the Tennessee River with plans to take over the land granted to the Tennessee Company at Muscle Shoals. On an island of the shoals, they constructed a blockhouse and a stockade, but The Glass, a Chickamaugan from Running Water, and sixty warriors forced them to abandon their attempt. Hubbard and his men would have been completely at the mercy of The Glass, who could have easily killed them. Instead, he told them to depart in peace. Taking no chance however, The Glass and his warriors reduced the structures to ashes.[155]

Initially, Hubbard, no doubt feared for his life. Brown, in Old Frontiers comments that Hubbard, following this incident, feeling shocked and angered, was probably surly about being outwitted by an Indian. It is wondered, though, if underneath this hardened exterior, he pondered the marvel of having his life spared by those who surely must have despised him.

The Cherokees were greatly stirred by the death of their beloved chief. "Almost every able-bodied warrior in the Nation hurr(ied) to join" the Chickamaugan "war camp."[156] Doublehead, mad with grief and reputed to be one of the fiercest Cherokee warriors on the frontier, [Figure 2.7] and his brother, Pumpkin Boy, made plans to avenge their brother's murder. Corn Tassel's nephew, Bob Benge, had his exploits recorded in Southwestern Virginia and Eastern Tennessee histories as a "near legendary figure of dread."[157] Another nephew, John Watts, usually humorous and witty, had always remained peaceful, but was so angered by the "crime against his peaceful uncle that he put himself" at the head of some two or three hundred warriors.[158] Even Corn Tassel's nephew, Sequoyah, for a period of time took up the war hatchet. A nephew had the relationship and loyalty to his uncle as that of a son to his father in Cherokee society. Kirk had murdered the "father" of many "sons."

The Old Cherokee law of avengement made it Corn Tassel's clan's duty to seek satisfaction for this injustice. Not only did these clan members have these legal rights, but Cherokee religious beliefs held that Corn Tassel's spirit could not move on to the next world until his murder had been avenged.

Despite these Cherokee warriors' intentions, they were outnumbered and suffered their losses as well. The battles dwindled down and three years later at the treaty held in Knoxville, Tennessee at White's Fort. John Watts, Jr., (sometimes referred to as Young Tassel), and his Chickamaugan warrior friend, Bloody Fellow, found themselves the chief speakers there. John Watts, fully aware of whose moccasins he now filled, spoke first:

> I know that the North Carolina people are headstrong. Under the sanction of a flag of truce, they laid low my uncle, (the Old CornTassel). It is vain for us to contend about a line. The North Carolina people will have their own way, and they will not observe orders of Congress or any body(sic) else..."[159] When you North Carolinians make a line, you tell us it is a standing one, but you are always encroaching upon it and therefore we cannot depend upon what you say.[160]

Governor Blount, argued,

> The lands were taken from the Cherokee in time of war, and I do not therefore consider the settlements to be encroachments.[161]

John Watts, Jr., known by now as one of the great orators of his people suddenly had no further use for words. His own mention of the beloved uncle evoked welling emotions. Bloody Fellow took over for him. John Watts stepped down. Tears misted in Young Tassel's eyes as visions of those he had lost surfaced in his mind over the lands of the "original people." It was an all too familiar argument. Watts was a mixed blood, but his heart belonged to the Cherokees. "Truth is," ...he heard his old uncle begin... "if we had no Land, we should have fewer enemies."[162]

WORKS CITED

Addington, Robert. *History of Scott County, Virginia*, Kingsport, Kingsport Press, 1932.

Alderman, Pat. *Nancy Ward, Cherokee Chieftainess/ Dragging Canoe, Chickamaugan War Chief*, Johnson City: Overmountain Press, 1978.

Brown, John P. *Old Frontiers: The Story of the Cherokee Indians from Earliest Times to the Date of Their Removal to the West*, Kingsport: Southern Publishers, 1938.

Calendar of Tennessee Papers,15-18.

Calendar of Virginia State Papers, 1785-1789 IV

Calloway, Brenda C. *America's First Western Frontier: East Tennessee*, Johnson City: The Overmountain Press, 1992.

Cherokee Phoenix, New Echota, Vol. I, 1828

Clanosee, Ancoo and the Tassell. *Draper Manuscripts 1XX45*, Wisconsin Historical Society, 1781.

[Corn Tassel] The Tassel, "Letter of The Tassell to the Commissioners." *Draper Manuscripts 1XX47*, Wisconsin Historical Society, 1781.

Debo, Angie, *A History of the Indians of the United States*. Norman: University of Oklahoma Press, 1970.

Ehle, John. *Trail of Tears, Rise and Fall of the Cherokee Nation*, New York: Doubleday, 1988.

Evans, E. Raymond. "Bob Benge." *Journal of Cherokee Studies I.2*, 1976.

Faragher, John Mack. Daniel Boone, *The Life and Legend of an American Pioneer*, New York: Henry Holt and Company, 1992.

Foreman, Grant. *Sequoyah*. Norman: University of Oklahoma Press, 1938.

Goodpasture, Albert V. "Indian Wars and Warriors of the Old Southwest, 1730-1807," *Tennessee Historical Magazine, IV*, 1918.

Haywood, John. *The Civil and Political History of the State of Tennessee from its Earliest Settlement Up to the Year 1796 Including the Boundaries of the State*, 1823, Knoxville: Tenase Company, reprinted 1969.

Henderson, Archibald. "The Treaty of Long Island of Holston, July 1777." *North Carolina Historical Review 8:55-116*, 1931.

The History of Tennessee, Washington D. C.: Goodspeed Publishing Company, 1886.

Kelly, James. "Attakullakulla," *Journal of Cherokee Studies 2.1*, 1976.

Kennedy, N. Brent. *The Melungeons, The Resurrection of a Proud People.*

Macon: Mercer University Press, 1994.

Kincaid, Robert L. *The Wilderness Road*. Harrogate: Lincoln Memorial University, 1990.

Lowrey, Major George. trans. Payne, John Howard, 1835, "Sequoyah or George Gist," *Journal of Cherokee Studies*, 1977.

Mails, Thomas E. *Cherokee People, The Story of the Cherokee from Earliest Origin to Contemporary Times*, Tulsa: Council Oak Books, 1922.

McFall, Pearl S. *The Keowee River and Cherokee Background*, Norman: University of North Carolina Press, 1940.

Milling, Chapman J. *Red Carolinians*. Chapel Hill: The University of North Carolina Press, 1940.

McKenny, Thomas L. and James Hall, *History of the Indian Tribes of North America*. Philadelphia Greenough [and] Rice & Clark, [1838-1844].

Mooney, James. *History, Myths, and Sacred Formulas of the Cherokees*. Asheville: Bright Mountain Books, 1992.

Mooney, James. "Myths of the Cherokee," *Smithsonian Institution Nineteenth Annual Report of the Bureau of Ethnology, Part 1*, 1900.

Moore, John Trotwood, ed. and Austin, P. Foster. *Tennessee, the Volunteer State 1769-1923*. The S. J. Clark Publishing Company, 1923.

Preston, Thomas W. *Historical Sketches of the Holston Valley*. Kingsport, Tennessee: Kingsport Press, 1926.

Ranney Letters, The. Ashfield Historical Society, 1851.

Ramsey, J. G. M., A. M., M. D. *The Annals of Tennessee*. Kingsport, Tennessee: East Tennessee Historical Society, 1823, reprinted by Kingsport, Tennessee: Kingsport Press, 1967.

Raulston, J. Leonard and Livingood, James W. Sequatchie, *A Story of the Southern Cumberlands*, University of Tennessee Press, 1974.

Satz, Ronald. *Tennessee's Indian Peoples from White Contact to Removal 1540-1840*. The Tennessee Historical Commission & The University of Tennessee Press, 1979.

Sharpe, J. Ed. *The Cherokees Past and Present*, Cherokee: Cherokee Publications, 1970.

Starr, Emmet. *Starr's History of the Cherokee Indians*. Oklahoma City, Oklahoma: The Warden Company, 1922.

Sutherland, Hetty S, ed. Sutherland, Elihu Jasper. *Pioneer Recollections of Southwest Virginia*. Clintwood: Mullins Printing, 1984.

Timberlake, Liet. Henry. ed. Williams, Samuel Cole. *Liet. Henry Timberlake's Memoirs*, Johnson City: The Watauga Press, 1927.

Williams, Samuel Cole. *Early Travels in Tennessee Country*

Williams, Samuel Cole. *Tennessee During the Revolutionary War.* 1944
    Knoxville: University of Tennessee Press, 1944, reprinted 1974.

Williams, Samuel Cole. *William Tatham, Wataugan.* Johnson City: The
    Watauga Press, 1947.

Woodward, Grace Steele. *The Cherokees.* Norman: University of Oklahoma
    Press, 1963.

NOTES

1   Samuel Cole Williams, *Tatham's Characters Among the North American Indians* was first published in *Annual of Biography and Obituary (London, 1820)*, and later in the United States, *William Tatham, Wataugan*, (Johnson City: The Watauga Press, 1947), p.104.

2   Albert V. Goodpasture, "Indian Wars and Warriors of the Old Southwest, 1730-1807," *Tennessee Historical Magazine*, IV, (1918), page 5.

3   Samuel Cole in *William Tatham, Wataugan*, op. cit., page 101. The author records William Tatham, who stated that Corn Tassel had "several friends of similar age and standing; of them it may suffice to mention Oconistoto and Onitossitah (sic), or the Corn Tassel." On page 103 of the same text, Tatham stated, "Onitositah, or the Corn Tassel, of the Cherokee nation of Indians, though somewhat younger, was the leading counsellor of Oconistoto, and consequently his contemporary, as well as that of Attakallahkallah (sic), Willanawaugh, and the Pigeon." Also, the "Chota Memorial" (See Figure 1.4), a joint effort by the Eastern Band of Cherokees, Tennessee Valley Authority and the Archaeological Placement Cooperative, the University of Tennessee and Jefferson Chapman, contains what is thought to be Oconsistota's grave (See Figure 2.6) and dates his birth 1710.

4   James Mooney, *Myths of the Cherokees and Sacred Formulas*, (1900 Nashville: Charles Elder, reprinted 1972). Smithsonian Institution Nineteenth Annual Report of the Bureau of Ethnology, Part 1, page 544.

5   Archibald Henderson, "The Treaty of Long Island of the Holston," *North Carolina Historical Review*, VIII, page 109.

6   Major George Lowery, 1835 trans. John Howard Payne, "Sequoyah or George Gist," *Journal of Cherokee Studies II;4* (Fall 1977), page 389.

7   John Trotwood Moore, *Tennessee, the Volunteer State*, (Chicago: The S. J. Clarke Publishing Company, 1923), page 193. Misspellings of the Cherokee original by the white pioneers may account for the different names too.

8   J. G. M. Ramsey, A. M., M. D., *The Annals of Tennessee*, (Kingsport: East Tennessee Historical Society, 1823, reprinted by Kingsport: Kingsport Press, 1967, page 304.

9   Mooney, op. cit., p. 544

10   Samuel Cole Williams, op. cit., page 103.

11   Mooney, op. cit., p. 544

12   Grant Foreman, *Sequoyah*, (Norman: University of Oklahoma Press, 1938), page 46.

13   Thomas E. Mail Mails, *Cherokee People, The Story of the Cherokee from Earliest Origins to Contemporary Time*, (Tulsa: Council Oak Books, 1992), page 79.

14   Ibid., page 72.

15   Ibid., page 72-73.

16   Albert V. Goodpasture, op. cit., page 3.

17   Archibald Henderson, op. cit., Corn Tassel asserted in one of his speeches "I live in Toque and my beloved people in Chote," page 81.

18   Albert V. Goodpasture, op. cit., page 6.

19   Henry Timberlake, *Liet. Henry Timberlake's Memoirs*, ed. Samuel Cole Williams, (Johnson City: The Watauga Press, 1927), pages 12-13.

20   Chapman J. Milling, *Red Carolinians*, (Chapel Hill: The University of North Carolina Press, 1940), page 339. Milling stated "Adairs, Wattses, Vanns, Rosses, Galphins, and McIntoshes were of the best Scotch (sic) and Irish blood."

21   Major George Lowrey, op. cit., page 47.

22   Ibid.

23   Three distant paternal relatives of the author, in interview, stated: 1. The old folks told that Chief Benge was the stepson of Virginia originator of Russell County Dorton's Fort 2. Another was told the same as a child by her mother. 3. His cousin informed that an uncle shared the story with him.Hetty S. and Elihu Jasper Sutherland's *Pioneer Recollections of Southwest Virginia*, a collection of interviews with southwestern Virginia residents in an account dated July 25, 1923, by Jonas Rasnick, a descendant of Lt. Vincent Hobbs (who shot Chief Benge) informed that "a white man named Dorton, who was wild and reckless and lived in the Indian Country.... was said to be the father of Benge, the chief of the Cherokees." He further stated that his uncle, Colonel Henson Hobbs, of Maryland..."told about these incidents, and I wrote it up for the *Lebanon News* (Lebanon, Virginia) and had L. L. Bays, the editor, print it some years ago." The article also states that "an uncle of Colonel Hobbs killed Benge....near Cumberland Gap. A Dorton, said to be a half-brother of Benge, was the leader of the whites...."

Family stories according to the author's distant cousin's family lineage was: When William Dorton, Jr., who was not in the particular group who pursued Benge, but pursued some of the Native Americans in band, and killed one of them, was asked why he didn't kill Benge, replied, "I couldn't have. He was my brother." Family stories continue in both lineages, where an actual connection in the family tree travel back at least five generations to William Dorton, Jr.'s sons, Joseph and Jacob. In addition, the daughter of one of the author's paternal relatives stated that she heard family stories that Benge would stand on the ridge above to protect Dorton's Fort, which housed his biological mother, the wife of William Dorton Sr., from other Indians. This would cause one to conclude that since the fort was noted to be singularly immune from Indian attacks, a rarity in that time period for that part of Virginia on the Wilderness Trail, the Benge-Dorton connection is plausible.

24   John Trotwood Moore, op. cit., page 228.

25   N. Brent Kennedy, *The Melungeons, The Resurrection of a Proud People*, (Macon: Mercer University Press, 1994), p. 28-29. According to Dr. Kennedy in a letter written to the author dated 10/23/94, he states, "It would appear that Benge has....some Melungeon connection, especially since Micajah Bunch [Benge] was "King of the Melungeons." Dr. Kennedy also expresses in his research the belief that Sequoyah's mother was of some Melungeon origin. This would raise the question of Corn Tassel's heritage being entirely full-blood Native American. According to Dr. Kennedy, the Melungeons infiltrated into and had a cultural influence on the Cherokee and Powhatan populations at an early date. In a lecture presented in Abingdon, Virginia, by Dr. Kennedy, he points out the dress of Sequoyah, the turban, etc. would be more characteristic of the Melungeon influence. In the author's research, Benge family genealogies relate Micajah is Bob Benge's uncle. While vacationing in Provo, Utah, this author met a South American Indian, an employee of a company that manufactures encapsulated herbs, with whom she engaged in conversation about the Indians of Peru, where the man originated. He stated, "You know, the South American Indians are descendants of the Israelites. They have a great promise in store for them." DNA results of those of Melungeon background have found South American Indian ancestry prominent. It is wondered by this author if this solves,

even without knowing why, the origin of the "Lost Tribe of Israel" claim prevalent among the old Melungeons. William Penn believed that the American Indians were descendants of the Lost Tribes of Israel. As mentioned earlier, Dr. Kennedy's belief that there is a strong Melungeon component among the Cherokee and Powhatan populations, would explain the claim for this descent.

26   The Ranney Letters, *Ashfield: Ashfield Historical Society*, 1851. This was a recorded ditty sung by white pioneers in the south around the time of the Georgia land lottery.

27   Robert L. Kincaid, *The Wilderness Road*, (Harrogate: Lincoln Memorial University, 1990), pages 97-98.

28   Ibid., page 98.

29   Ibid., pages 99-100.

30   Brenda C. Calloway, *America's First Western Frontier: East Tennessee,* (Johnson City: The Overmountain Press, 1992), Page 92.

31   Samuel Cole Williams, *Tennessee During the Revolutionary War,* (Knoxville: University of Tennessee Press 1944), page 63.

32   John P. Brown, *Old Frontiers* (Kingsport: Southern Publishers, Inc., 1938), page 168.

33   Ibid., pages 168-169.

34   Ibid., page 169.

35   Ibid., page 170.

36   Ibid.

37   Ibid.

38   Ibid.

39   Ibid., page 170-171

40   Samuel Cole Williams, *Tennessee During the Revolutionary War*, (1944 Knoxville: The University of Tennessee Press), reprinted 1974, page 63.

41   Ibid.

42   Archibald Henderson, op. cit, page 84.

43   Samuel Cole Williams, *William Tatham, Wataugan*, op. cit., page 101.

44   John Haywood, *The Civil and Political History of the State of Tennessee from its Earliest Settlement Up to the Year 1796 Including the Boundaries of the State*, (1823, Knoxville: Tenase Company, Reprint 1969), page 505. "Uku" or "ouka" refers to the head man.

45   Samuel Cole Williams, *Tennessee During the Revolutionary War,* op. cit., page 67.

46   Ibid., page 210.

47   Samuel Cole Williams, *William Tatham, Wataugan*, op. cit., page 101.

48   Archibald Henderson, op. cit., pages 60-61.

49   Samuel Cole Williams, *Tennessee During the Revolutionary War,* op.cit., page 67.

50   Ibid.

51   Ibid., page 66.

52   Samuel Cole Williams, *William Tatham, Wataugan*, page 101.

53   Ibid.

54   John Haywood, op. cit., page 505.

55   J. Ed. Sharpe, *The Cherokees Past and Present*, Cherokee: Cherokee Publications, 1970), page 13. Information is given about the dress of the Cherokee peace chief. "Moccasins with small bells attached….cap of otter skin covered with white crane feathers…. strings of deer hoofs around the ankles and a wand of swan wings" were among the items of the chief's dress.

56   Samuel Cole Williams, *William Tatham, Wataugan*, page 104.

57   Ibid.

58   Archibald Henderson, op. cit., pages 66-68.

59   Ibid., page 72.

60   Ibid., page 74.

61   Ibid., page 69.

62   Ibid, p. 66-68 Corn Tassel asserts in one of his speeches at The Treaty of Long Island, that he gave the string to insure truthfulness ("….that you may tell the truth.) Pearl S. McFall also states in *The Keowee River and Cherokee Background,* that the person presenting a string of white beads expressed a wish for peace and mutual happiness.

63   Samuel Cole Williams, *William Tatham, Wataugan*, op. cit., page 108.

64   Archibald Henderson, op. cit., page 70-80.

65   Ibid., page 82.

66   Ibid., page 81.

67   Ibid.

68   Samuel Cole Williams, *William Tatham, Wataugan*, page 108.

69   J. Ed. Sharpe, op. cit., page 13.

70   Samuel Cole Williams, op. cit., page 109.

71   Ibid.

72   Archibald Henderson, op. cit., page 89.

73   Ibid., page 90.

74   Henry Timberlake, op. cit., page 76.

75   Archibald Henderson, op. cit., pages 91-92.

76   Ibid., page 92.

77   Ibid., pages 93-94. Corn Tassel, in his speech, refers to the Pidgeon (sic) who in 1762 travelled "over the Great Water" to England with Timberlake. The Pidgeon (sic) escorted Gist back to Virginia following the treaty. George Lowrey, one of the traders to whom he refers, married Lucy Benge, sister of Bob and Martin "The Tail" Benge, who both married Lowrey's sisters. The Lowreys were a prominent family, and Sequoyah resided with George Lowrey's family for a time. *Starr's History of the Cherokees* genealogical information traces the Lowrey family to Nannie of the Holly Clan, who married the Scots trader, John Lowrey.

78   Ibid., pages 100-101.

79   Ibid., page 102.

80   Ibid.

81   Ibid., page 95.

82   Ibid., page 95-96.

83   Samuel Cole Williams, *William Tatham, Wataugan*, op. cit., page 104.

84   Ibid.

85   Archibald Henderson, op. cit., pages 107.

86   Samuel Cole Williams, *William Tatham, Wataugan*, op. cit.,page 104-107. (William Tatham stated that the speech "is supposed to have been bereaved of much of its native beauty by the defects of interpretation; for the manly and dignified expression of an Indian orator loses nearly all its force and energy in translation."

87   Ibid., page 77.

88   Ibid., pages 107-108.

89   Ibid.

90   Samuel Cole Williams, *Tennessee During the Revolutionary War,* 1944, page 199.

91   Letter of the Tassell to William Christian, William Preston, Arthur Campbell, Joseph Martin, Evan Shelby, Joseph Williams and John Sevier, Commissioners, July 27, 1781. *Draper Manuscripts* 1XX47, Wisconsin Historical Society, Microfilm copy.

92   Letter of Clanosee, Ancoo and the Tassell to Col. Joseph Martin and Col. William Christian, at Col. Martin's house. July 26, 1781, *Draper Manuscripts* 1XX45, Wisconsin Historical Society, Microfilm Copy.

93 Samuel Cole Williams, op. cit., page 201, quoting the *General Greene Papers* in Manuscript Division of the Library of Congress.

94 Letter of Col. William Christian to Cherokee warriors and chiefs, July 28, 1781 *Draper Manuscripts* 1XX49, Wisconsin Historical Society, Microfilm copy.

95 Pat Alderman, *Nancy Ward, Cherokee Chieftainess, Dragging Canoe, Cherokee Chickamaugan War Chief,* (Johnson City: The Overmountain Press), 1978, page 66.

96 Moore, op. cit., page 192 quoting State Records of North Carolina, Vol. 11, page 654.

97 J. G. M. Ramsey, A. M., M. D., *The Annals of Tennessee* (Kingsport: East Tennessee Historical Society, 1823, reprinted by Kingsport: Kingsport Press, 1967) page 304-305.

98 Ibid., page 271.

99 Ibid.

100 John Trotwood Moore, op. cit., page 192.

101 Ibid., page 162.

102 Ramsey, op. cit., page 305.

103 Ibid., pages 304-305.

104 Ibid., page 305-306.

105 Ibid., page 319.

106 Ibid., page 306-307.

107 Ibid., page 308.

108 *The History of Tennessee*, (Goodspeed Publishing Company, 1886), page 85.

109 Emmett Starr, *Starr's History of the Cherokees* (Oklahoma City: The Warden Company, 1922), page 55.

110 Chapman J. Milling, op. cit., page 324.

111 Ibid.

112 Emmett Starr, op. cit., page 35.

113 Pat Alderman, op. cit., page 67.

114 Ibid., page 67-68.

115 Ibid., page 68.

116 Ibid.

117 Pearl S. McFall, 1938, *The Keowee River and Cherokee Background*, 1938. (Norman: University of Oklahoma, reprinted 1959), page 68.

118 Brown, *Old Frontiers*, op. cit., page 249-250.

119 Pat Alderman, op. cit., page 69.

120 Ibid., page 69.

121 Ibid., page 69.

122 Chapman J. Milling, op. cit., page 325.

123 Ibid., page 324.

124 Angie Debo, *A History of the Indians of the United States*, (Norman: University of Oklahoma Press, 1970), page 72.

125 John Trotwood Moore, op. cit., page 194.

126 Ramsey, op. cit. pages 343-344.

127 Ibid., p.344-345

128 Ibid., p. 344

129 Ibid.

130 Ibid., p. 346.

131 Corn Tassel, *Calendar of Virginia State Records,* 1785-1789 IV, page 306.

132. Ibid, pages 306-307.

133 Ibid. page 306.

134 Archibald Henderson, op. cit., page 66.

135 Samuel Cole Williams, *William Tatham, Wataugan*, op. cit., page 103.

136 John Trotwood Moore, op. cit., page 194.

137 John P. Brown, op. cit., page 276.

138 *The History of Tennessee*, op. cit., page 87.

139 John P. Brown, op. cit., page 227 quoting *North Carolina State Records,* 22:695.

140 Haywood, op. cit., page 195.

141 Emmett Starr, op. cit., page 35.

142 John P. Brown, op. cit., page 277

143 Ibid.

144 Ibid.

145 Ibid.

146 Major George Lowrey, op. cit., page 46.

147 Ibid.

148 John Haywood, op. cit., page 196.

149 J. P. Brown, op. cit., page 278.

150 Ibid.

151 John Trotwood Moore, op. cit., page 131

152 Ibid.

153 Ibid.

154 Haywood, op. cit., page 518.

155 John Trotwood Moore, op. cit., page 196.

156 John Brown, Old Frontiers, op. cit., page 278.

157 A. V. Goodpasture, op. cit., p. 257

158 John Trotwood Moore, op. cit., page 204.

159 *Cherokee Phoenix*, New Echota, Vol. I, No. 26, p. 1, August 27, 1828

160 Ibid.

161 Ibid.

162 *Calendar of Virginia State Papers*, IV, page 306. Chief Corn Tassel, uncle of John Watts, Jr., wrote in June 1787 to Virginia's Governor Randolph: "I observe in every treaty that we have made that a bound is fixed but that your people settle much faster shortly after a treaty than before....Truth is, if we had no lands, we should have fewer enemies."

ILLUSTRATIONS

Figure 1.0   *Seven Cherokee Delegates to London in 1730*, an engraving by Isaac Basire.

Cherokees who decided to accompany Attakullakulla to England to ensure his safety. Sir

Alexander Cuming, Scottish adventurer to America, brought this group before King George III

in London, England in 1730. Here, they made friendship agreements and found themselves

courted as allies in trade and war with Britain. They evoked much curiosity and attraction while

in London. (*National Anthropological Archives, Smithsonian Institution*)

Figure 1.1   Conocotocko, Standing Turkey or "Cunne Shote," a relative of Corn Tassel, was one of three to travel to London with Henry Timberlake in 1762. London, 1762. *The Gilcrease Institute of American History and Art*, Tulsa, Oklahoma.

SE-QUO-YAH

Figure 1.2   Sequoyah, Inventor of the Cherokee Syllabary from McKenney, Thomas L. and
James Hall. *History of the Indian Tribes of North America*. Philadelphia: Greenough [and] Rice
& Clark, 1838.

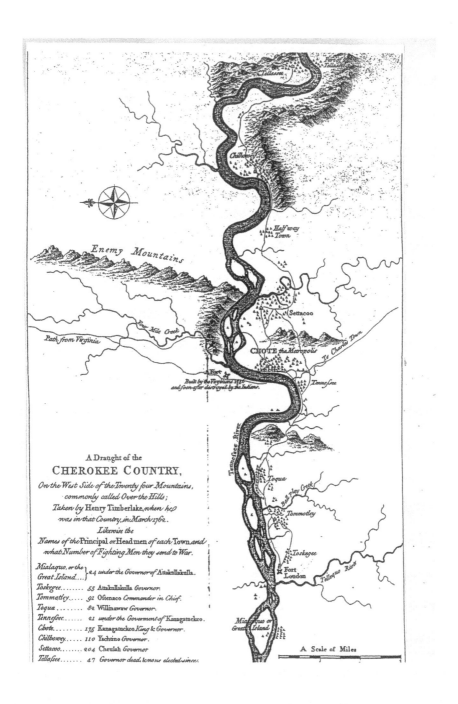

Figure 1.3   Henry Timberlake, emissary from the British Colonies to the Overhill Cherokees, illustrated this map of the Cherokee villages on the Little Tennessee River, 1762.

Figure 1.4   Above: Path to the Chota Memorial

Below: The Chota Memorial to the Cherokees of the Little Tennessee Valley, a
joint effort by the Eastern Band of Cherokees, Tennessee Valley Authority and the
Archaeological Placement Cooperative, The University of Tennessee and Jefferson
Chapman. Each monument pays homage to one of the seven clans.
(photographs by the author)

Figure 1.5   Houston Benge Tehee, a prominent descendant of Martin "The Tail" Benge, as
pictured *in Starr's History of the Cherokees*, by Emmett Starr, served as Registrar of
the Treasury of the United States.

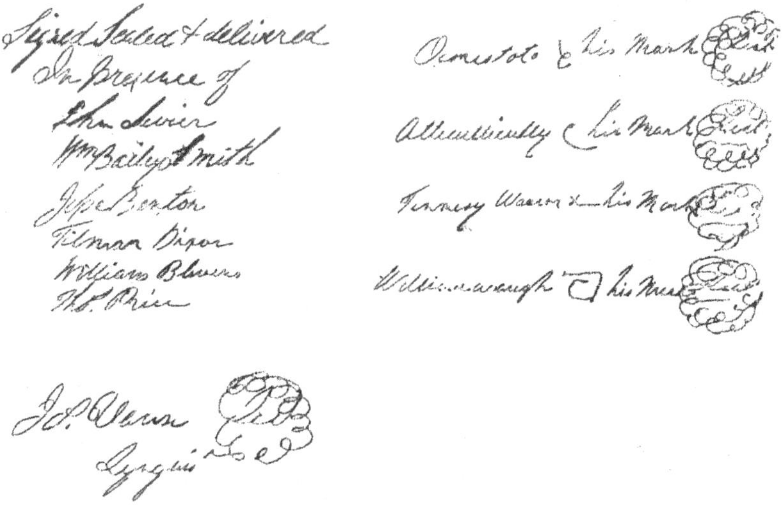

Figure 1.6   The Watauga Purchase at Sycamore Shoals Signers, March 19, 1775. The original is in the *Tennessee State Archives*. Signers:

John Sevier   Oconistoto   his mark   Seal

Wm. Bailey Smith   Atticullicully   his mark   Seal

Jessee Benton   Tennessy   Warrior   his mark   Seal

Tilman Dixon   Willinawaugh   his mark   Seal

William Blevins

Thomas Price

Figure 1.7   Daniel Boone Escorting Settlers Through the Cumberland Gap by George Caleb

Bingham, Washington University Gallery of Art, St. Louis, 1852

Figure 1.8   The Cherokees exit on the Trail of Tears some years after Corn Tassel's

death. John Benge, a descendant of Corn Tassel's nephew, Martin "The Tail" Benge, was leader

of the Cherokees during this sorrowful event.

The Trail of Tears by Robert Lindneux, 1942. Woolaroc Museum, Bartlesville, Oklahoma

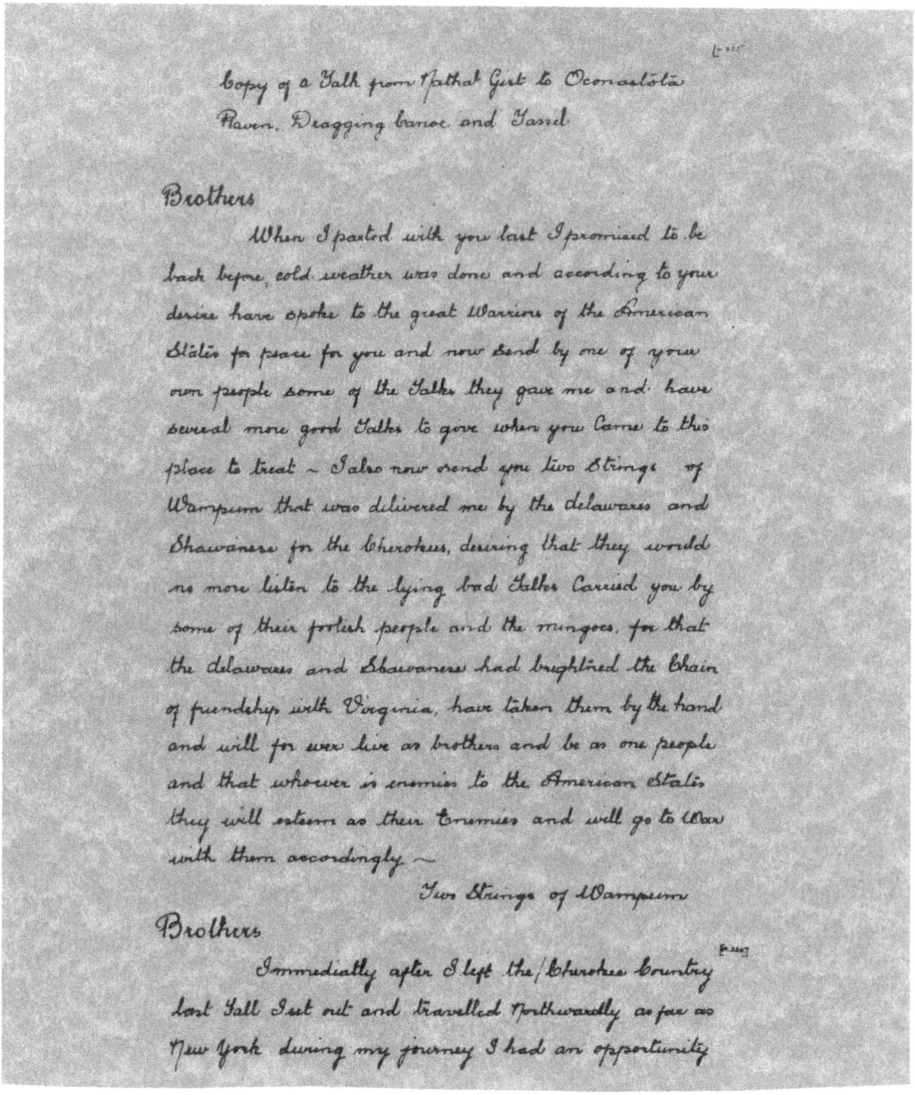

Copy of a Talk from Ifathal Gist to Oconastota
Raven, Dragging Canoe and Tassel

Brothers

When I parted with you last I promised to be
back before cold weather was done and according to your
desire have spoke to the great Warriors of the American
States for peace for you and now send by one of your
own people some of the Talks they gave me and have
several more good Talks to give when you come to this
place to treat ~ I also now send you two Strings of
Wampum that was delivered me by the Delawares and
Shawanese for the Cherokees, desiring that they would
no more listen to the lying bad Talks carried you by
some of their foolish people and the mingoes, for that
the Delawares and Shawanese had brightened the Chain
of friendship with Virginia, have taken them by the hand
and will for ever live as brothers and be as one people
and that whoever is enemies to the American States
they will esteem as their Enemies and will go to War
with them accordingly ~

Two Strings of Wampum

Brothers

Immediatly after I left the Cherokee Country
last fall I set out and travelled Northwardly as far as
New York during my journey I had an opportunity

Figure 1.9   This copy, inviting the chiefs to the Treaty of Long Island, is thought to be
Dragging Canoe's. It was located in the *British Archives* in London by Williams and published in
Tennessee During the Revolutionary War, 1944.

of seeing and talking with many great Council ones
and Warriors of America and now know their hearts
is good to all the Red people their Neighbours if it is not
their own fault — At last near New York I met with
my old friend General Washington at the head of a great army
seen great numbers of prisoners he had taken of the people
over the great Water at war with us and know that
the King during the Cold Weather has lost four thousand five hundred men near New York before I left
that and I do think they are all killed and taken before
now as they were then surrounded in a little Spot Starv-
ing for bread and begging for peace —
All my Brothers listen attentively

I saw the great English Warriors Letter to
General Washington begging peace as the French
and Spaniards had begun a War over the great
Water and that their Ships must go home to fight
and save the Country where the King lives —
Brothers

If you now mind well what I say all may
be well with you yet. I seen plenty of powder, Lead
and other goods in Virginia and you may get enough
after the peace is Confirmed and I think I can get
the white people to forgive the / Murder you committed
the last Winter as I hope it was done by some foolish
young men Contrary to the advice of the Head men.

You know all particularly my Comrade the Dragging Canoe that what I advised last year before you went to War was for your good, and would have saved the lives of many of your people; and saved your Towns from being destroyed —

Now I again tell you this year it will be much worse than last unless you now make a peace when the good time is come, as it is the last offer of peace you will get from Virginia; so don't blame me when hard times comes again among you as I have now told you the truth and advised you for your good and now offer to shake hands with all my Brothers the Cherokees in behalf of Virginia —

The bearer hereof or a runner sent from you with a white flag must come to me here in twenty days that I may know whether you are coming for peace or not, they shall be kindly treated and kept from harm

(Signed) Nathl Gist

Great Island Fort
25th March 1777

Endorsed Great Island Fort / 25th march 1777 / Copy of a Talk from / Nathl Gist at Oconastota / & other head Men of the / Cherokees — / In Mr Stuarts (No 17) of / 15th June 1777.

Figure 2.0   Chief George Lowrey, brother-in law of Corn Tassel's grand nephews, Bob and

Martin Benge, who married Lowrey's sisters. George Lowrey married Bob and Martin's sister,

Lucy Benge. Sequoyah lived with George and Lucy Lowrey for a time. A comical story is told of

a time when Chief Lowrey went to Washington, D. C. representing the Cherokees. While dining

with dignitaries, Lowrey, in reference to someone there, who disregarded the Indians as savages

who lived on wild roots and berries, asked (pointing to the sweet potatoes) if

some "roots" might please be passed to him. (George Catlin, *Thomas Gilcrease Institute of*

American History and Art, Tulsa)

Figure 2.1   Speech of Corn Tassel (as translated) to the Commissioners, July 27, 1781 (Calendar of Tennessee Papers of the Draper Manuscripts, 15-18).

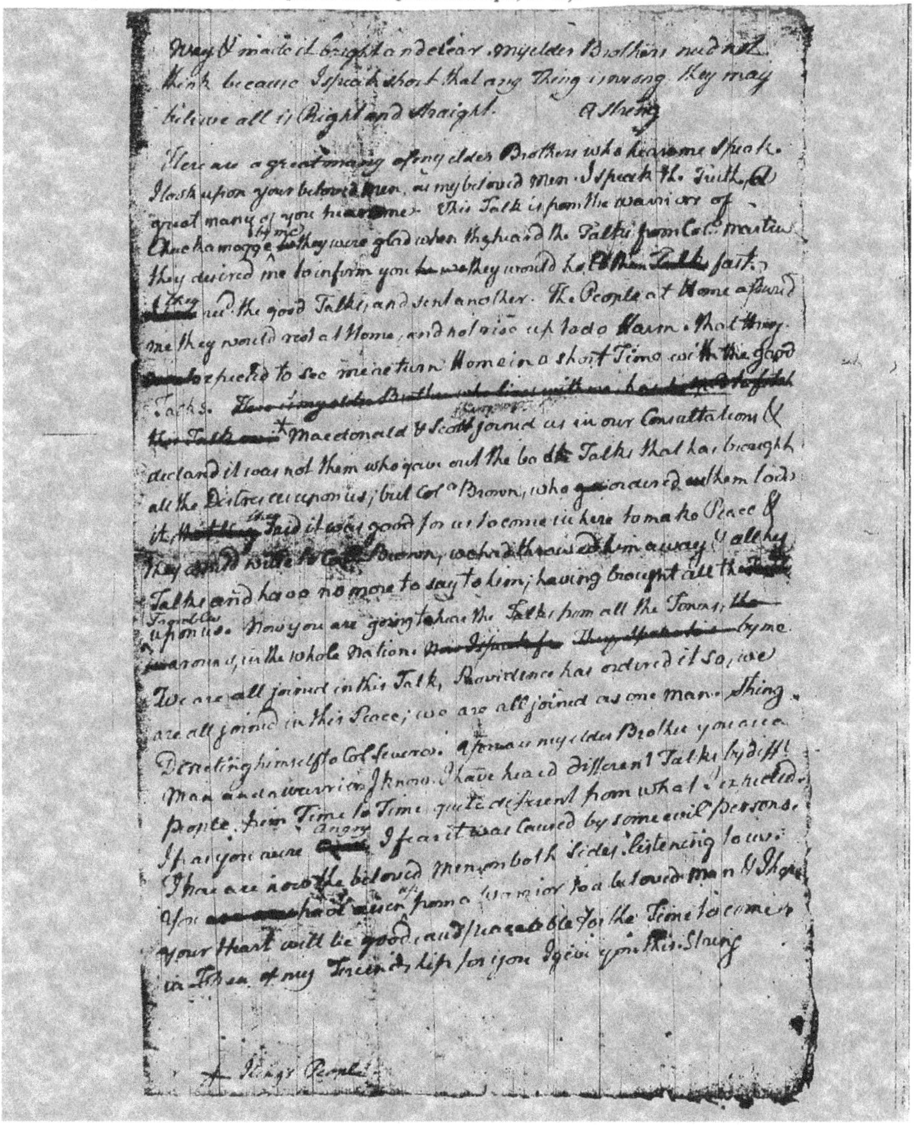

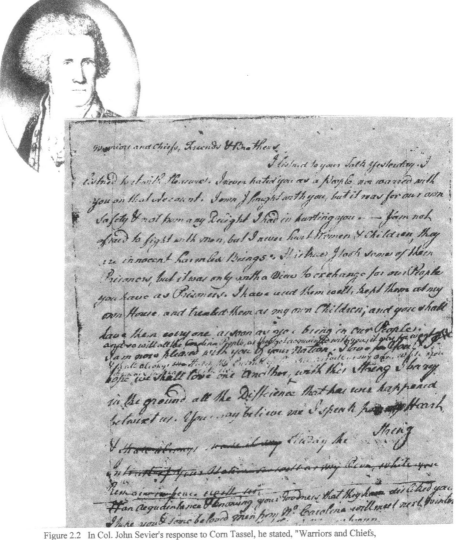

Figure 2.2   In Col. John Sevier's response to Corn Tassel, he stated, "Warriors and Chiefs,

Friends and Brothers..." (*Draper Manuscripts* 1XX47, July 1781) Colonel John Sevier, who was

later governor of Tennessee, led an active campaign against the Cherokees (*Tennessee State*

Library and Archives).

Figure 2.3   Reacting to Nancy Ward's "Mother's" Speech. "You know that women are always looked upon as nothing; but you are our sons. Our cry is all for peace; let it continue. This peace must last forever. Let your women's sons be ours; let our sons be yours. Let your women hear our words." After hearing her speak, the commissioners let the Cherokee retain some of their lands. This is the original translation of Col. Christian's reply. (*Draper Manuscripts*)

Figure 2.4   Holston River from Site of Treaty of Long Island (photograph by the author.)

Figure 2.5   Footbridge over the Holston Leading to the Site of Treaty of Long Island

(photograph by the author)

Figure 2.6　　Grave of Oconastota, War Chief (other spellings: Oconistota, Oconostoto, etc. His name translated Groundhog Sausage). His grave was identified by the dugout canoe Colonel Joseph Martin had written about in which he buried this chief. (photograph by the author) Oconistota was Corn Tassel's "friend of similar age and standing." Corn Tassel was "the leading counselor and a chief speaker for Oconistota. He succeeded Oconistota in the principal chiefship." (Samuel Cole Williams in *William Tatham, Wataugan*).

Figure 2.7   Doublehead, Corn Tassel's brother, lives on through this marker, which does not

include any political reasons from the Cherokee perspective. Surely, the white man could be said

to be "savage" in the atrocities that were not recorded, but it is never written on markers this

way. Doublehead married Sarah Priber, Christian Priber's (a German lawyer who tried to

establish a utopia among the Cherokees) daughter.

Figure 2.8   Treaty of Long Island Memorial in present day Kingsport, Tennessee pays

homage to the seven clans (photograph by the author). This is the site where ancient chieftains

met and smoked their pipes of peace.

Figure 2.9   A stone monument to the Wataugans marks the original location of the fort where the Treaty of Sycamore Shoals was signed in present day Elizabethton, Tennessee (photograph by the author).

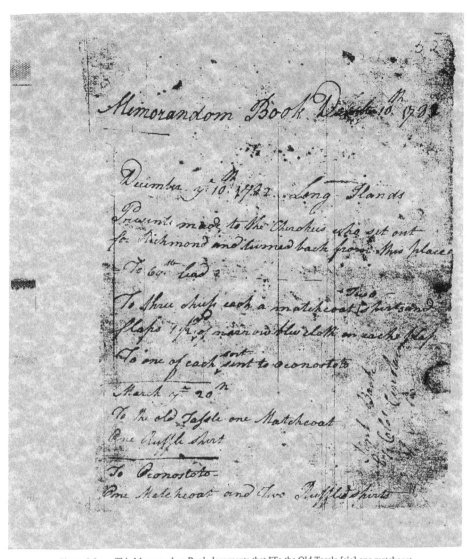

Figure 3.0   This Memorandum Book documents that "To the Old Tassle [sic] one matchcoat

and one ruffled shirt was given at "Long Islands." To Oconostoto - One Matchcoat and Two

Ruffled shirts [sic]. (*Draper Manuscripts*)

Figure 3.1   The Sequoyah Birthplace Museum in present day Vonore, Tennessee

(photograph by the author). There is a burial mound nearby which holds unidentified graves of

Cherokees found during excavations as Chota was to be flooded over by Tennessee Valley

Authority in building a dam.

Figure 3.2   Tecumseh, the famous Shawnee leader, who tried to form an intertribal

Confederacy to halt the encroachments on Native American territories. Tecumseh's brother,

Chiksika, who was killed in battle fighting alongside the Chikamaugans, was especially revered

by Corn Tassel's grandnephew, Chief Bob Benge. Benge as well as Corn Tassel were of some

Shawnee heritage. Merely speculating, could there be a hereditary link between the two families

of these Shawnee and Cherokee greats? (*National Anthropological Archives, Smithsonian*

Institution).

Figure 3.2   Tanasi, once capital of the Cherokee nation, was located next to Chota. This

memorial to the town from which the state of Tennessee took its name reads:

"The site of the former town of Tanasi, now underwater, is located about 300 yards west of this

marker. Tanasi attained political prominence in 1721 when its civil chief was elected the first

"emperor of the Cherokee Nation." About the same time, the town name was also applied to the

river on which it was located. During the mid-18th century, Tanasi became overshadowed and

absorbed by the adjacent town of Chota, which was to the immediate north. The first recorded

spelling of Tennessee as it is today, occurred on Lt. Timberlake's map of 1762 (See Figure 1.3

near middle, right side)

     In 1796, the name Tennessee was selected from among several as most appropriate for

the Nation's 16th state. Therefore, symbolized by this monument, those who reside in this

beautiful state are forever linked to its Cherokee heritage. It was erected by the *Tennessee*

Historical Commission Foundation and the Tennessee Valley Authority (photograph by the

author)

Captions

Figure 1.0   *Seven Cherokee Delegates to London* in 1730, an engraving by Isaac Basire. Cherokees who decided to accompany Attakullakulla to Englad to ensure his safety. Sir Alexander Cuming, Scottish adventurer to America, brought this group before King George III.

Figure 1.1   Conocotocko, Standing Turkey or "Cunne Shote," a relative of Corn Tassel, was one of three to travel to London with Henry Timberlake in 1762. *The Gilcrease Institute of American History and Art,* Tulsa, Oklahoma, 1762.

Figure 1.2   Sequoyah, Inventor of the Cherokee Syllabary from McKenney, Thomas L. and James Hall, *History of the Indian Tribes of North America.* Philadelphia: Greenough [and] Rice & Clark, 1838.

Figure 1.3   Henry Timberlake, emissary from the British Colonies to the Overhill Cherokees, illustrated this map of the Cherokee villages on the Little Tennessee River.

Figure 1.4   Above: Path to the Chota Memorial
Below: The Chota Memorial to the Cherokees of the Little Tennessee Valley, a joint effort by the Eastern Band of Cherokees, Tennessee Valley Authority and the Archaeological Placement Cooperative, the University of Tennessee and Jefferson Chapman. Each monument pays homage to one of the seven clans (photographs by the author).

Figure 1.5   Houston Benge Tehee, a prominent descendant of Martin "The Tail" Benge, as pictured in *Starr's History of the Cherokees*, by Emmett Starr, served as Registrar of the Treasury of the United States.

Figure 1.6   The Watauga Purchase at Sycamore Shoals Signers, March 19, 1775. The original is in the *Tennessee State Archives.*
Signers:

John Sevier	Oconistoto his mark Seal
Wm. Bailey Smith	Atticullicully his mark Seal
Jessee Benton	Tennessy Warrior his mark Seal
Tilman Dixon	Willinawaugh his mark Seal
William Blevins	
Thomas Price	

Col. Christian's reply. (*Draper Manuscripts*)

Figure 2.4   Holston River from Site of Treaty of Long Island (photograph by the author)

Figure 2.5   Footbridge over the Holston Leading to the Site of Treaty of Long Island (photograph by the author)

Figure 2.6   Grave of "Oconastota," War Chief (other spellings: Oconistota, Oconostoto, Oconistoto, etc. His name translated Groundhog Sausage. His grave was identified by the dugout canoe Colonel Joseph Martin had written about, in which he buried this chief. (photograph by the author) Oconistota was Corn Tassel's "friend of similar age and standing." Corn Tassel was the leading counselor" and a chief speaker for Oconistota. He succeeded Oconistota in the principal chiefship." (Samuel Cole Williams in *William Tatham, Wataugan*)

Figure 2.7   Doublehead, Corn Tassel's brother, lives on through this marker, which does not include any political reasons from the Cherokee perspective. Surely, the white man could be said to be "savage" in the atrocities that were not recorded, but it is never written on markers this way. Doublehead married Sarah Priber, Christian Priber's (a German lawyer who lived among the Cherokees) daughter.

Figure 2.8   Treaty of Long Island Memorial in present day Kingsport, Tennessee pays homage to the seven clans (photograph by the author). This is the site where ancient chieftains met and smoked their pipes of peace.

Figure 2.9   A stone monument to the Wataugans marks the original location of the fort where the Treaty of Sycamore Shoals was signed in present day Elizabethton, Tennessee (photograph by the author).

Figure 3.0   This Memorandum Book documents that "To the Old Tassle one matchcoat and one ruffled shirt was given at Long Islands." To Oconostoto One Matchcoat and Two Ruffled shirts (sic). (*Draper Manuscripts*)

Figure 3.1   The Sequoyah Birthplace Museum in present day Vonore, Tennessee (photograph by the author). There is a burial mound nearby which holds unidentified graves of Cherokees found during excavations as Chota was to be flooded over by Tennessee Valley Authority in building a dam.

Figure 3.2   Tecumseh, the famous Shawnee leader, who tried to form an intertribal Confederacy to halt the encroachments on Native American territories. Tecumseh's brother, Chiksika, who was killed in battle fighting alongside the Chikamaugans, was especially revered by Corn Tassel's grandnephew, Chief Bob Benge. Benge as well as Corn Tassel were of some Shawnee heritage. Merely speculating, could there be a hereditary link between the two families of these Shawnee and Cherokee greats? (*National Anthropological Archives*, Smithsonian Institution).

Figure 3.3   Tanasi, once capital of the Cherokee nation, was located next to Chota. This memorial to the town from which the state of Tennessee took its name reads: "The site of the former town of Tanasi, now underwater, is located about 300 yards west of this marker. Tanasi attained political prominence in 1721 when its civil chief was elected the first "emperor of the Cherokee Nation." About the same time, the town name was also applied to the river on which it was located. During the mid-18th century, Tanasi became overshadowed and absorbed by the adjacent town of Chota, which was to the immediate north. The first recorded spelling of Tennessee as it is today, occurred on Lt. Timberlake's map of 1762 (See Figure 1.3 near middle, right side). In 1796, the name Tennessee was selected from among several as most appropriate for the Nation's 16th state. Therefore, symbolized by this monument, those who reside in this beautiful state are forever linked to its Cherokee heritage." It was erected by the *Tennessee Historical Commission Foundation and the Tennessee Valley Authority* (photograph by the author).

Mitzi Dorton is a multi-genre writer, a former postsecondary learning specialist and educator. As an adult, she often hung out in history rooms of local colleges. It was there in some antiquated books, that she found herself introduced to Chief Corn Tassel. Samuel Cole Williams, historian in *William Tatham, Wataugan*, complained that other than James Mooney's description, there was "no other sketch of this able chief." Dorton travelled to the old Cherokee towns and various treaty sites, acquainting herself further with his background. By the time she reached Chota, Chief Corn Tassel was simply the hand of an old friend felt along the path, and she wanted to share his story.

Mitzi has been published in the literary journals, *Rattle* and *Rubbertop Review*. She was part of an award-winning anthology, *Rise, an Anthology of Change*, with *Northern Colorado Writers*, which received the *Colorado Book Award* in this category. Her work has been featured in *Proud to Be, Southeast Missiouri State University Press, Poems from the Lockdown, Willowdown Books, Cinematic Short Story Contest, 2020 Tunnel of Lost Stories, Wingless Dreamer*, and others. Her manuscript was a finalist for *The Totally Free Best of the Bottom Drawer Global Writing Prize* competition, *Black Spring Press*. She now lives on a mountaintop in upstate New York, where she enjoys birds, nature and quilting stories.

CPSIA information can be obtained
at www.ICGtesting.com
Printed in the USA
BVHW021441100722
641714BV00007B/128